THE LIGHT BULB STRATEGY
7 Steps to Switch It On and Lead a Brilliant Life

Maureen & Gilles,
Lead with Brilliance!

ROBERT CRAIG

THE LIGHT BULB STRATEGY

7 Steps to Switch It On and Lead a Brilliant Life

The author and publisher specifically disclaim any liability resulting from the information contained in this book. Always consult a professional when seeking medical, financial or legal advice.

Copyright © 2015 by Robert Craig

All rights reserved.

Published by 10-10-10 Publishing

No part of this book may be reproduced or transmitted in any form or by any means, electronic or mechanical, including photocopying, recording, or by any information storage and retrieval system, without permission, in writing, from the author.

Cover Design – Matthew Craig

Many images contained in this book
(including book cover images) – Dollar Photo Club

Author portrait by Vine Images Inc. Julie Johnson Photography

ISBN: 978-1-928155-62-1

PRAISE FOR THE LIGHT BULB STRATEGY

"Robert gives you a NEW 'Light' approach to personal development – His creative and unique Light Bulb Strategy Blueprint provides the framework to help you plan and lead a brilliant life."
- **Jack Canfield,** Bestselling author of *The Success Principles* and the *Chicken Soup for the Soul* series

"Robert shows you how to unlock your potential, remove your roadblocks and really shine with brilliance in everything you do."
- **Brian Tracy** - Author, *Eat That Frog*, and *No Excuses*

"I found the 7 step Light Bulb Strategy Blueprint easy to understand and simple to follow. I suggest you follow *The Light Bulb Strategy* to design your personal development plan."
- **Jeffrey Tam,** Award winning author of *Retire Wealthy: Make More Money, Pay Less Tax, Protect Your Assets*

"To live a brilliant life, use *The Light Bulb Strategy* Blueprint as a tool to guide you to live with intention, discover your passion, address your fears and reflect on the things that truly inspire you. Robert – continue to be the light and illuminate the way for people to find their path to lead a brilliant life."
- **Betty Jean Hendricken** RN, BScN (Dist.) Clinical Nurse Specialist

"In *The Light Bulb Strategy*, Robert turns you into a light bulb – metaphorically. Then he shows you how to change your thinking, plan your future and execute your plan so that you can lead a brilliant life – a must read!"
- **Maureen Richardson,** School Teacher

"Robert's book, *The Light Bulb Strategy*, helps you focus your light on what is truly important to lead a brilliant life."
- **Zoltan Vitai,** Investor and Entrepreneur

To my wife, Andrée, my best friend and love of my life. And to my sons, Matthew, Kevin and Nicholas, the three main reasons why I am so inspired. And to the memory of my Mom and to my Dad, my hero.

Contents

Acknowledgements   ix

Foreword   xi

Introduction   1

Step:

1   Change Your Light Bulb   13

2   Envision Your Light Bulb of the Future   35

3   Power-up Your Light Bulb   55

4   Build Yourself a Better Light Bulb   77

5   Protect Your Light Bulb   101

6   Switch-on Your Light Bulb   115

7   Reflect on the Brilliance from Your Light Bulb   125

ACKNOWLEDGEMENTS

I want to thank my parents for providing all their guidance and love. I lost my mother last year. She inspired me to always do my best, to pursue my passion and find true love – I miss her dearly. My father is my hero – he taught me about discipline, focus and having strong values. The support he gave my mom while she was sick was incredible. His dedication to her was an example of what true love is all about.

I want to thank my beautiful wife, Andrée. She is my best friend and love of my life. She was so supportive all through the process of writing this book. She is my best critic and fan. She inspires me every day.

My three sons - Matthew, Kevin and Nicholas are the reasons why I work so hard to improve myself. They also inspire me every day.

And to Raymond Aaron for his incredible brilliance. He inspired me to write this book in the first place. For that I am so grateful. His guidance, direction and support helped me so much. I also want to thank Jennifer Le from the Raymond Aaron Group for her support in getting my book published. And to Lisa Browning for editing and making my book look brilliant. Thank-you so much.

FOREWORD

The Light Bulb Strategy by Robert Craig gives you the blueprint to help you lead a brilliant life. In his book, Robert walks you through his 7 step process using his unique *Light Bulb Strategy Blueprint*. This visual blueprint drawing of an actual light bulb provides you with the framework for creating and executing your life plan. You wouldn't build a house without a blueprint, why should designing your life be any different?

Robert's book takes you to your very core to get you to understand who you are, what you want to do with your life and why you want to do it. Then he shows you how to develop your plan, execute it and then reflect on your brilliance.

All throughout the book, Robert uses "light" analogies which makes the concepts easy to understand, apply and remember. It also makes it fun to read!

If you are serious about your personal development, read this book. After reading it, you will never look at a light bulb the same way again.

Raymond Aaron
New York Times Bestselling Author

INTRODUCTION
The Path to "The Light Bulb Strategy"

This book is about brilliance – your brilliance. It's about leading your life in such a way that you find your brilliance, grow it and share it with others. It's about reaching your potential; having a fulfilling life and helping others do the same. However, brilliance doesn't just happen on its own. You need to plan for it - strategically.

"Strategy" sounds complicated and it can be. When we hear the word "Strategy", we conjure up images of great military leaders planning their moves against an enemy; the deployment of troops and military hardware. We also think of great sporting events like football or hockey and how to break through the other team's defenses to score goals and win the game.

A strategy is simply an overall plan of action which provides a method to identify your purpose, understand your values, set and achieve your goals in a world with limited resources.

We live in a very complicated world - too complicated! As Richard Branson says, "Complexity is the enemy. Any fool can make something complicated. It's hard to make something simple."

That is the purpose of *The Light Bulb Strategy* – to take a complicated subject – designing your life to be brilliant and making it simple to understand.

So first, let me tell you about myself as I continue my journey to lead a brilliant life. I have an incredible wife who I adore, three great boys and a wonderful lifestyle. I have had many successes in my life and certainly have had my share of failures. I am thankful for both. They have taught me many lessons and have allowed me to grow as a person.

As I write, I am working for one of the largest corporations in Canada. I have had many roles within the company and have learned a great deal. I have held roles in Training, Operations, Marketing and Strategy.

During my time in both Training & Operations, I worked to improve our operating procedures. The unfortunate thing about operating procedures is that they are often very dry reading. They are to-the-point step-by-step documents that serve a very specific purpose.

One of my greatest passions is learning new things and then sharing my knowledge with other people so that we can all add value to the organization. I took our operating procedures and brought them up to a new level by developing training modules that provided better context for the procedures that followed. I called it Wholesale University - a series of PowerPoint presentations grouped into modules that simply explained how the Wholesale business worked in our company. When you have better understanding, you get better execution. Now, when people join the Wholesale group or want to learn more about the Wholesale business, they are referred to me to provide them with the Wholesale University content. I have been referred to as "The Prof. of Wholesale", "The Dean" and once was called...Yoda! I wasn't sure how to take that one!

In my role in Marketing and Strategy, I utilized the strategic planning process. My most recent project was to lead the development and execution of a national proprietary credit card program which has been very successful. The process is very

The Light Bulb Strategy

in depth. Every stone needs to be over-turned to ensure the best approach is taken.

As part of the process you need to ensure you maximize the use of limited resources. One of those limited resources is people.

The company I work for recognizes that one of its greatest assets is its people. Unfortunately, people don't get listed on the balance sheet of a corporation. The assets listed on a balance sheet include such things as cash, investments, buildings and equipment. To support the growth of the company, they make many investments – including developing their people. Every person within the company has a set of goals to achieve each year - for the business and for their own personal development. For me, my personal development goals were (and still are) to continue to develop my project management and communication skills and more specifically how to provide better explanations.

I am a personal development enthusiast. I read a lot on personal development, listen to audio programs and attend conferences and courses. The amount of information out there on how to improve ourselves is incredible and can be overwhelming.

The challenge is that we may read great books or take engaging courses and feel inspired, but then we settle back into our daily routine and don't put into practice our new learnings. Maybe it's due to overload! "It's too much to take in all at once" or "I know I should do it, but I just don't have time." When our brains are overloaded - they tend to shut down and we revert back to our comfort zones.

Things are complicated because often they are simply not explained properly. Communication of key ideas and concepts is lost because we can't get our brains to grasp and hold onto the material we need to succeed.

Just the other day I ran into one of my colleagues in the lunchroom and asked him how he was doing applying the concepts we learned in a recent course we attended together. "Not so good, I need to go back to the material and refresh myself. I don't remember off the top of my head what the key concepts were of that model we were taught." To remember better, we need to do some extra work with our brains, but the extra effort is worth the investment of time. Let me explain.

Our brains work in mysterious ways. We can remember things better when we learn to use the visual power of our brains. Our brains learn well with images - they provide better context so we can remember things better. I read that we actually process images 60,000 times faster than reading text - A picture really is worth a thousand words.

Let me give you an example on how our brains work well with visuals. This is a technique I learned from an Accelerated Learning course I took from author and speaker Brian Tracy.

Here is a list of 10 things:

1. Apple
2. Pizza
3. Car
4. Mattress
5. Dog
6. Windshield
7. Flower
8. Shovel
9. Hockey Puck
10. House

The Light Bulb Strategy

Now, close the book and write down the words you remember. You will remember some of the words, but probably not all of them.

Here is a system you can use to quickly memorize this list of words. If someone gives you the number, you can give them the word. And if they give you the word, you can tell them the number.

The trick is to use visualization! Okay, to do this you need to create anchor words for the numbers 1-10. Here are the anchor words I was taught - they rhyme with the number, more or less.

1. Run
2. Zoo
3. Tree
4. Door
5. Hive
6. Sticks
7. Heaven
8. Gate
9. Wine
10. Den

So let's take number 1 - Run. One (1) and run rhyme. Memorize one (1) and run - pretty simple - our brains can handle that.

Now, the next step is to visualize yourself running in your mind's eye. What I do is close my eyes and visualize myself running down the street in front of my house. Pick a place that you are familiar with and visualize yourself running there.

Next step - now that you see yourself running, insert the word you are trying to memorize - in this case the word was "apple" and incorporate that item into your visualization. Visualize yourself running with an apple in your hand. To make the visual stronger which will help you memorize the word better, eat the apple while you are running - feel the juice running down your chin, the feel of the crunchiness in your mouth.

Next word - Two (2) - Zoo. I visualize a large gorilla sitting in a cage at the zoo. What is he doing? Eating pizza! He's got a large pizza box and is snorting while he consumes the slices. See the pepperoni on the triangular slice as he puts it into his mouth.

Next word - Three (3) - Tree. Get an image of a tree in your mind - make it memorable. Now insert your word into your image - car - How in the world did a car get stuck in the branches of a tree?!! Visualize it! Come up with your own visualization of the car and the tree.

Next word - Four (4) - Door. I visualize the front door to my house. Think of a door that is familiar to you; it could be your apartment door, your bedroom door, or your office door. Pick one and make it memorable. Again - insert your word to remember - mattress. I visualize myself struggling to get a large mattress through my front door...Got it!

Next word - Five (5) - Hive. That's right, a bee hive - visualize that bee hive. There are bees all around it! Now insert your next word into your visual - dog. That poor dog is being chased by bees! He's barking, running around in circles. Visualize it - how does it make you feel? How can you help the dog get away from the bees?

The Light Bulb Strategy

Next word - Six (6) - Sticks. Branches on the ground from a tree, drum sticks whatever type of sticks you want to remember. Now bring in your word - windshield - visualize sticks sticking through the windshield of a car. To make it more vivid - imagine them in your own car if you have one.

Next word - Seven (7) - Heaven - Think of the sky and imagine your word rising up into the clouds - the word is flower - visualize flowers popping out of the ground and floating up into the clouds.

Almost there...

Next word - Eight (8) - Gate - think of a gate going into a backyard, a gate into a stadium. Now visualize your word - shovel - think of a shovel leaning up against your gate or entering a stadium gate and having to carry a shovel along with your tickets to get in.

Next word - Nine (9) - Wine - think of a glass of wine - I think you get it by now. The word is puck - visualize a hockey puck sitting in your glass of wine. Who put that there?! You ruined a perfectly good glass of wine!

Last word - Ten (10) - Den - I think of my desk in my office den at home and then I visualize the item being on my desk - the word is house - visualize a miniature model of a house sitting in the middle of your desk.

Okay - now after you have practiced to memorize your rhyme words for each number and then visualize your rhyme word with the word you are memorizing, you will amaze yourself at how many of the words you can remember.

This is a great trick to impress your friends or colleagues of your great memory skills. Now when my wife sends me to the grocery store she kids me by saying. One - Run - Milk. Think of drinking milk while you run to the store! Nice!

Another key thing I learned was the power of simplicity. Simplicity helps us remember things better. In their book, "Made to Stick", brothers Chip and Dan Heath explain the power of using analogies. "Analogies make it possible to understand a compact message because they invoke concepts you already know."

So, I took something simple - that people know about and can easily visualize - a light bulb. We already use the light bulb today as a symbol of thinking or idea generation. Have you ever seen an image of a person with a light bulb over their head? So I took this concept and developed it further to come up with "The Light Bulb Strategy" - an explanation strategy so that you can create a simple plan to lead a brilliant life. In this case, the light bulb represents you - metaphorically!

You're a Light Bulb...

So let's talk about the light bulb in real simplistic terms. I think we all know what a basic incandescent light bulb looks like. (See the Light Bulb Diagram). It has a metal screw base with an electrical contact point. Coming out of the screw base, the light bulb has a glass dome. Housed within the glass dome, there are contact wires that connect to a filament that glows and produces light when in contact with the low pressure inert gas. The wires and filament are supported by a glass support base.

The Light Bulb Strategy

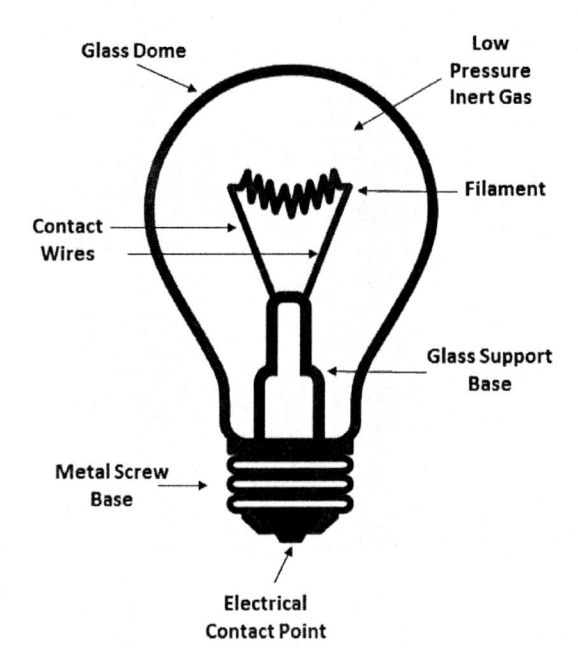

Diagram of a light bulb with labels: Glass Dome, Low Pressure Inert Gas, Contact Wires, Filament, Glass Support Base, Metal Screw Base, Electrical Contact Point.

So now you're thinking: How does a light bulb represent me and how can it help me to understand and remember what I need to do to create a plan on how to lead a life that's brilliant? That's where *The Light Bulb Strategy Blueprint* comes into play.

The Light Bulb Strategy Blueprint is a visual model. It shows the 7 steps required to create a plan to help you lead a brilliant life. Here are the steps:

Step 1 – Change Your Light Bulb

This step is represented by the base of the light bulb. It is all about understanding our core – it's WHO we are; our personalities, our values, our beliefs, our habits, our fears. We need to understand ourselves; have self-awareness and be prepared to make the necessary changes to get on the path of brilliance. We need to change our thinking – Think Brilliance!

Step 2 – Envision Your Light Bulb of the Future

This step is represented by the outer casing of the light bulb – the grooves. This is where we get clarity on WHAT we want to do – daily, monthly, annually, and for the rest of our lives! It's about defining our vision, our mission and our goals and ensuring they are all aligned. We want to develop rich grooves and not get stuck in a rut!

Step 3 – Power-up Your Light Bulb

This step is represented by the metal contact point at the bottom of the light bulb. This is where you connect with your power source – WHY power. Here we define WHY we want to achieve our goals, vision and mission in life. It also defines power drivers that provide energy to power up our light bulb.

Step 4 – Build Yourself a Better Light Bulb

This step is represented by the glass stem that comes up from the base of the light bulb. This is where we define HOW we are going to achieve our vision. Here we determine our strategy and create a plan using our limited resources as efficiently as possible.

Step 5 – Protect Your Light Bulb

This step is represented by the glass globe of the light bulb. Inside the globe is the space we live in – our environment. This is where we define WHERE we will get our big things done. The glass globe itself represents time – time is limited. It's about WHEN we are going to get those big things done. This step is

The Light Bulb Strategy

all about protecting our environment, protecting our time in order to achieve what we want in life.

Step 6 – Switch-on Your Light Bulb

This step is represented by the two wires that extend up from the glass stem and attach to the filament. One wire represents your personal life; the other, your professional or work life. At this step, you are executing your plan and working to keep balance between your personal and professional life. When you achieve balance with these two wires, your filament glows. The better the EXECUTION of your personal and professional work life, the brighter the filament glows!

Step 7– Reflect on the Brilliance from Your Light Bulb

This step is represented by the actual glow of the Light Bulb. Here we will look at the levels of brilliance - the better the execution towards achieving your goals, vision and mission, the brighter your Light Bulb shines! The more brilliant you get your Light Bulb - the happier you will be as you will be living a more fulfilled life. This is where you also reflect on your brilliance and understand how your new experiences work back to add more to the base of your Light Bulb. And then the cycle repeats itself...

In the chapters that follow, I will get into more detail on how these concepts all come together to help us develop a plan for future success. I will throughout the book tie in "LIGHT" analogies to help further explain "The Light Bulb Strategy" with some supporting tactics. As well, there will be "Brilliance in Action" exercises to help you work through your plan.

So let's get started and LIGHT 'em Up! - Your Light Bulb that is!

The Light Bulb Strategy Blueprint

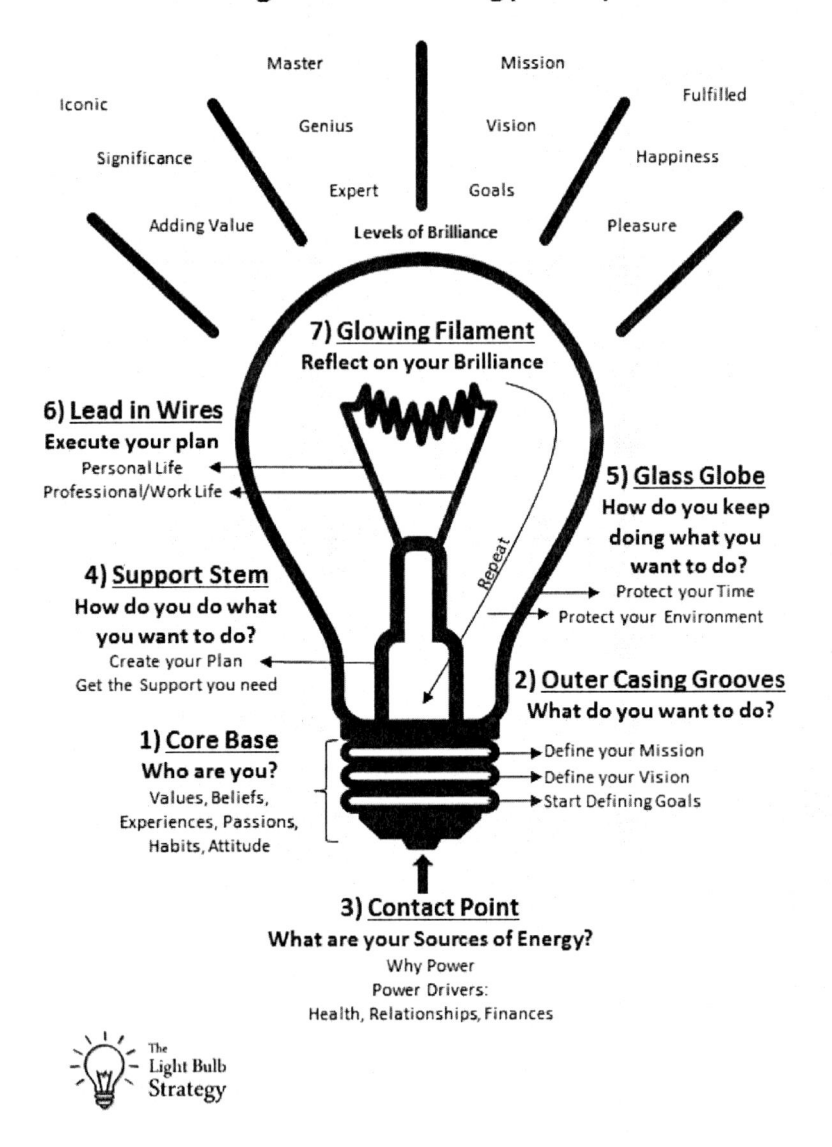

Levels of Brilliance (rays emanating from bulb):
- Iconic
- Master
- Mission
- Fulfilled
- Significance
- Genius
- Vision
- Happiness
- Adding Value
- Expert
- Goals
- Pleasure

7) Glowing Filament
Reflect on your Brilliance

6) Lead in Wires
Execute your plan
- Personal Life
- Professional/Work Life

5) Glass Globe
How do you keep doing what you want to do?
- Protect your Time
- Protect your Environment

4) Support Stem
How do you do what you want to do?
- Create your Plan
- Get the Support you need

2) Outer Casing Grooves
What do you want to do?
- Define your Mission
- Define your Vision
- Start Defining Goals

1) Core Base
Who are you?
Values, Beliefs, Experiences, Passions, Habits, Attitude

3) Contact Point
What are your Sources of Energy?
Why Power
Power Drivers:
Health, Relationships, Finances

The Light Bulb Strategy

1

The Light Bulb Strategy Blueprint

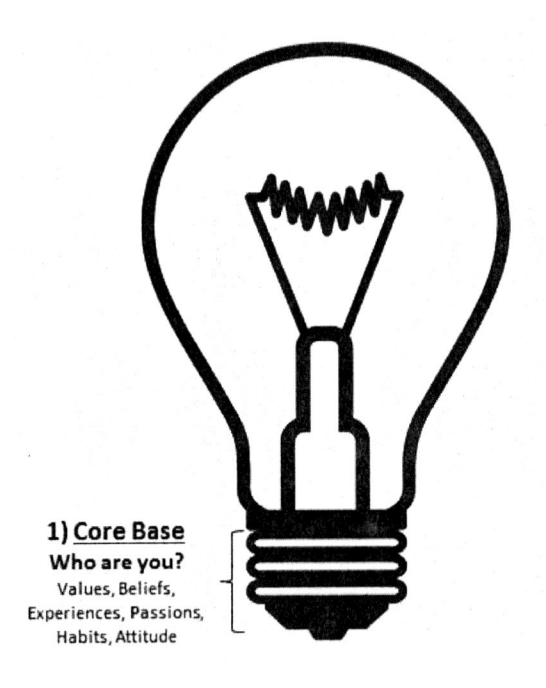

1) Core Base
Who are you?
Values, Beliefs, Experiences, Passions, Habits, Attitude

The Light Bulb Strategy

"To confront a person with their own shadow is to show them their own light."

Carl Jung

Step 1

CHANGE YOUR LIGHT BULB

"Change your Thinking – Think Brilliance!"

You must have heard the one - "How many psychiatrists does it take to change a light bulb? Just one, but the light bulb has to want to change!"

Do you want to change? Do you want to improve, grow and develop yourself? Do you want to lead a brilliant life and achieve your dreams? If you want your life to change - **You** must change! But in order for change to occur you must make a choice to change and be totally responsible for making that change.

When you change a light bulb – you replace it. You take the old one out and replace it with a new one. For our Light Bulb Strategy metaphor, changing the light bulb doesn't mean replacing yourself – that can never be done as you are irreplaceable! It means changing the way we think. Changing the way we talk to ourselves, the way we visualize and the way we behave. We need to be positive, we need to think about how to find our brilliance, keep it, grow it and share it – **"Think Brilliance. Become Brilliant."**

Life is all about making choices. Every day we make choices that determine the trajectory our lives take. Make consistently good choices (brilliant choices) and life will be rewarding. Make consistently bad choices and life will be disappointing and miserable.

Do you have a plan for your life so you can be happy and fulfilled? Do you know where you are headed? Do you know how to get where you want to be in life? Do you know your purpose in life and why you were put on this earth?

The first step of "The Light Bulb Strategy" is to change your light bulb by understanding WHO you are and making the necessary changes to get on the path to brilliance.

A key starting point in building a strategy is collecting information. We need to review and understand this information so we can make some key decisions. This information will help us to determine our current state, illuminate our true purpose and define our values. This process of information gathering provides us with greater self-awareness. As author and leadership guru Robin Sharma says, "With better awareness, we make better choices and with better choices we get better results."

Your Inner LIGHT of Brilliance

On "The Light Bulb Strategy Blueprint", your center core – your inner light is represented by the base of the light bulb. The core is WHO you are. Your character is formed and developed over time from your beliefs, thoughts, religion, attitude, experience, education, upbringing and habits – just to name a few... and because of this each of us is unique and different from one another - there is only one you!

The important thing is to be self-aware of your core - to understand where you are coming from; what you truly value today. Your values come from your core and are very important to understand. Have you ever stopped to think about what it is that you truly value? Have you ever written your values down? Your values help you make decisions by providing direction on how you want to operate in the world.

Family, Security, Freedom, Continuous Learning and Honesty are some of the key values that I hold today. These core values set the baseline on how I function in the world. These values give me my navigational direction in life.

The LIGHT at the end of the Tunnel

One of my top values is Security - having a safe community for my family (my top value) to live in and having a secure source of income to provide for my family.

When I came out of university with my Bachelor's Degree in Economics, I got my first job working for a small advertising agency as a junior account executive. The job was fascinating - working on television commercials, sitting in studios working on radio voice over commercials, attending creative meetings to review marketing strategies to meet client's requirements. It was very exciting - but within a couple of months, I was let go. I was devastated.

My next job was "a little safer" - working with a medium sized franchise company that had retail stores in shopping centres across the country. I worked in the finance department as a Retail Audit Clerk - which meant I reviewed and validated store transaction paperwork to ensure accuracy and that all the money from sales that was supposed to get to the bank did get into the bank.

It was during this job that I got to build on my university education and got a further understanding on how financials of a company work - Income Statements, Balance Sheets, Cash Flow Statements and Business Plans. I moved into a new role as a Business Development Manager where I worked with Franchisees to build business plans so they could get financing for their operations from the banks. Later, I was promoted to Retail Controller within the finance department. It was in this role I could see that the business was struggling. Was there light at the end of the tunnel? Yes, but it was indeed a freight train - not good. It was just a matter of time.

Then one day, two cars pulled into the company driveway. All employees were called to the common area of the accounting department. The gentlemen introduced themselves as Trustees in Bankruptcy. They read a list of people that were to leave the premises immediately. People who I had been working with for years (like my second family) were told to leave. There was a whole myriad of emotions that filled the room - anger, fear, frustration, disbelief. People hugged each other; tears flowed while others out of anger formatted their hard drives on their computers.

I was asked to stay to work under the Trustee in Bankruptcy - to wind down the company. I wasn't sure how long that assignment would last. As I worked under the Trustee, I looked for other work. I was looking to get into an even larger company - one that could provide even greater security – if that truly exists!

Well I did land a job at a very large national company. During my time at the company, we have gone through some major restructurings and even a merger. There were some very tense moments as I waited to hear if I would keep my job.

The Light Bulb Strategy

What does all this have to do with my value of security? Well it showed me that no matter what size company you work for, there is no true job security. If I truly valued security as one of my core values, then it would make sense that I create a backup plan should something happen with my job. I will talk about this later on in the book.

All of my work experiences have become part of my core – they have contributed to building my base – my "Inner Light of Brilliance". These experiences have provided me with learnings - something to reflect on to allow me to make course corrections going forward. Good or bad, these experiences have also helped me grow as a person.

As I mentioned earlier in the introduction, there will be some exercises to action so that we can work on our brilliance. These "Brilliance in Action" exercises will help you take the steps you need to build your overall plan.

<u>Brilliance in Action</u>:

Exercise – Define Your Current Values:

As part of the first step to understand yourself, you need to be clear on your current values.

Take out a piece of paper and write down 10 of your most important values.

What in life is most important to <u>you today</u>?

These will serve as your inner compass to provide you with direction moving forward. Your values will help you make decisions as part of The Light Bulb Strategy going forward.

The Dimmer Switch – Our Habits

A dimmer switch allows you to adjust the amount of power that affects the brilliance of a light bulb. When the dimmer switch is on full - it provides maximum power to the light bulb. When it's at the lowest setting, the light is very dim and may even be turned off.

"The Dimmer Switch" in our light bulb metaphor, represents our habits and has a great impact on the amount of brilliance given off by our light bulb. If we have positive habits, it provides greater power to our light bulb – more brilliance. Negative or bad habits can drain the power to our light bulb – less brilliance. Too much negative energy if not managed properly, could burn out our light bulb for good!

The Dimmer Switch

Positive Habits

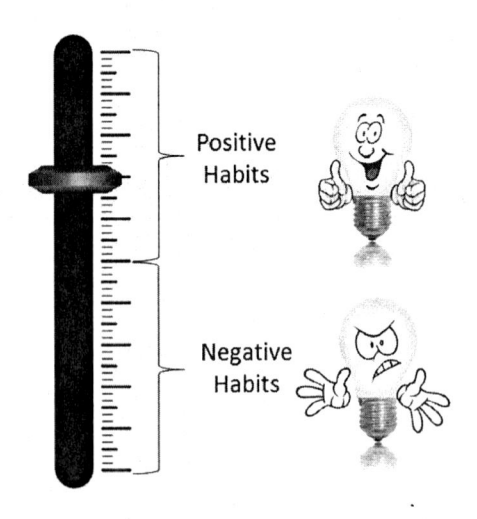

Negative Habits

The Light Bulb Strategy

Habits, good or bad are developed over time. They are formed by the choices we make over and over again. These repeated behaviors which are stored in our basal ganglia (in the center of our brain) over time become automatic. It gets to a point where we don't even realize we are doing them. The brain creates these automatic routines to save energy.

To be successful, we must change our habits and develop "Habits of Brilliance" that create positive energy for our light bulb. We need to replace our bad habits with positive ones and get them built into our every-day routines. When they become part of our regular routines, they will become automatic.

Aristotle once said, "We are what we repeatedly do. Excellence, then, is not an act, but a habit."

You must keep focus and discipline to get and keep positive habits in place. I've heard some experts say that it takes about 21 days to form a new habit. I'm not sure where that number comes from, but I do know that each of us are different and it will take time to build habits into our routines so they become automatic.

To break bad habits you must first be aware of them. Awareness is a key step to start replacing bad habits with good ones. When you have awareness you can put in place an action plan to make corrections.

For example, I must admit, I'm a nail biter- always have been. I bought an App called Habit Master. The app allows you to track daily routines with your smart phone. I started to track the number of days I could go without biting my nails. The App brought greater awareness to my nail biting because it would bring it to my attention daily when I used my smart phone. I would check off day after day if I did not bite my nails.

I also used the app to help me drink more water, take time to read, prepare my gym bag the night before so it is ready for me to take when I rush out the door to work in the morning. If it's not ready to go out the door, then it gives me an excuse not to go to the gym at lunch time, "I was in too much of a hurry to get out the door" – a bad excuse. The app helped me change my behavior and drive new processes.

Author Charles Duhigg writes in his book, *The Power of Habit*, "To modify a habit, you must decide to change it. You must consciously accept the hard work of identifying the cues and rewards that drive the habits' routines and find alternatives. You must know you have control and be self-conscious enough to use it." It's not about "Will-Power" – as you can't always count on that. It's about consciously making a choice to change that specific habit.

Charles goes on to talk about the process of the three-step loop that forms a habit. There is the cue which serves as a trigger to get your brain to do something automatically. Then there is the routine – what you do. And then there is the reward – why your brain decides the habit is worth repeating.

Let me give you an example of how the habit loop works by talking about traffic lights...

Traffic LIGHTS

If you drive a car, you know red traffic lights signal you to slow down and stop. We have learned this behavior – a red light is a cue that triggers us to execute a certain action in our brain – to slow down and stop. Once you see the red light, your brain automatically tells you to take your foot off the gas and apply the brakes (the routine). What's the reward? Simple – you avoid

The Light Bulb Strategy

getting into an accident – pure survival instincts. If you have been driving long enough, this routine has become a habit. Our brain has done this process over and over again. So much so that it gets locked into our basal ganglia part of the brain – the part of the brain where our habit routines live. To change or replace a bad habit, you need to change the cue, the routine or the reward.

The opposite of a red light is a green light. The green light triggers us to go; to start doing something, to accelerate. When you are sitting at a red light and it turns green (the cue or trigger), you automatically take your foot of the brake and apply the gas, looking both ways of course before proceeding (the routine). Then you are on your way to your destination (the reward).

I'm going to take red lights and green lights a step further – they can be our reminders (our triggers or cues) when we think about our habits in general.

What habits can you apply "Red Light Thinking" to? That is, what habits do you need to stop or slow down? For example, maybe you need to stop smoking? Maybe you need to eat less fast food? Maybe you need to stop being a victim?

What habits can you apply "Green Light Thinking" to? That is, what habits do you need to start doing? Maybe you need to start exercising? Maybe you need start reading more? What good habits should you continue doing? Perhaps you're already great at reading with your kids at night before bedtime. Perhaps you have a good habit of drinking water during the day. Perhaps you have good eating habits.

The other light we haven't talked about yet is the amber light – that light that signifies that the light is changing from green to red. It cautions us that change is coming and we need to make the right call – to make a decision to slow down and stop or proceed with caution. You need to make a decision here – you can't do just nothing!

What events can you apply "Amber Light Thinking" to? That is, what events in your life is the world sending you alerts about? Perhaps your child comes home with a black eye, your spouse shows up late again, you feel excessively tired all the time? Do you take action on these types of "amber alert events" in your life or do you turn a blind eye to them? Do you retreat to your comfort zone so as not to rock the boat? You need to take action on these events.

Brilliance in Action:

Exercise – Become Aware of your Habits

Identify habits in your life that you need to apply "Red Light Thinking" to?

What habits do you need to slow down or even stop doing?

What actions can you take to slow down or stop doing this habit? What system could you put in place to develop a "Habit of Brilliance"?

Identify habits in your life that you need to apply "Green Light Thinking" to?

What habits do you need to start, do more of or continue doing?

What actions can you take to start, do more of or continue doing this habit? What system could you put in place to develop a "Habit of Brilliance"?

The Light Bulb Strategy

Identify events in your life that you need to apply "Amber Light Thinking" to? What alerts is the world sending you that you need to address?

Adjusting the LIGHT

A very important thing about the dimmer switch is that it should be adjusted gradually in small increments. Changing habits take time, especially if you have had this habit for a long time. Let's say, for example you are going to change your exercise habits. So, you decide you will go to the gym every day for 3 hours. It sounds great but the challenge will be that it will be very difficult to sustain that level of activity. You may start off strong, but gradually your willpower will fade and you will go back to your old ways.

Our bodies need time to adjust gradually to avoid shocking the system. Have you ever been sound asleep when someone came into the room and turned on the light suddenly? - It's a shock to the system!

Do you listen to music in your car? Have you driven along increasing the volume as you drive? Then you pull into your driveway, turn off the car and go inside your home. Then, the next time you come out to the car and start the ignition - the music comes on blaring - scaring you half to death! It is the same high volume you were listening to before - you just haven't had a time to adjust to the loud sound. When you listened to your stereo before you were aware you were making it louder and your body was able to prepare and adjust for it.

Work on only changing a few habits at a time – if you try to do too much you could quickly become overwhelmed – Adjust the light gradually.

Work on adjusting your identified habits daily – to ensure you are replacing bad habits with "Habits of Brilliance". It will take time, but getting our habits right is critical to leading a brilliant life.

Throughout this book, as we go through the steps of *The Light Bulb Strategy*, the dimmer switch will play a major role in determining how brilliantly we can get our light bulb to shine. There are many more habits to discuss!

Our Fear of the Dark

One of the major obstacles that holds us back in life is our fears. They can prevent us from achieving our goals, realizing our vision and ultimately rob us from achieving our mission in life.

We all have fears - all of us. There is no escaping this fact. Some fear the dark, public speaking, fear of failure or even success. The unfortunate thing is that we let our fears control us. Fear can paralyze us, stop us in our tracks, and limit us from living up to our true potential. We need to change how we think about fear.

In her book *The Fear Cure*, Lissa Rankin, M.D., talks about two kinds of fear - true fear and false fear. The true fear is actual fear we feel when a real life incident happens in our life, while false fear is fear that is imagined. She says, "True fear is a

The Light Bulb Strategy

natural survival mechanism, here to protect you, and false fear is an important teaching tool, here to enlighten you. Fear affects every one of us. It's nothing to hide. On the contrary, it is worth examining so it can point you toward a better way to live, a way that aligns you with your natural courage and supports you in optimal health."

It is in our core that we fear - as humans that is the way we have been built - to survive. Our reptilian brain takes over - to fight, freeze or flee. And when I mean take over - instead of using our thinking brain (our pre-frontal cortex), the reptilian part of our brain becomes dominant.

The reptilian brain in our head controls the most basic functions of survival such as breathing, digestion and movement, but it also controls our fight or flight response. We used our reptilian brains more when we as a human species spent most of our time in survival mode - running from predators and hunting for food. The good thing is that in today's society, we don't spend as much time in pure survival mode (at least I hope you don't). We don't need to use our reptilian brain as much. Although we don't use it as much, it still can dominate if we don't know how to control it. The great thing about being human is that we can control our reptilian brain, - just by being more aware of it. When we see that we are reacting to fear, by being aware of that reaction to fear, we can better control it.

A simple example of this is driving a car. - If you drive, sooner or later someone is going to cut you off - it's inevitable. Now, when that happens, your reptilian brain reacts and before you know it you might be out to seek revenge - foul language, finger gestures, yelling; you may even have the urge to race ahead and cut that person off yourself. This is where you stop, pause and let your thinking brain take control again. "Wow, did that ever frustrate me and make me angry" - then let it go.

Our reptilian brains manifest our fears and tells us to cling to the known - to stay in our comfort zone. And while we are comfortable there, it's like we are holding a blanket up over our heads in bed (which blocks our brilliance); we cannot grow and develop. We no longer need to let our reptilian brains dominate our thinking – we have light (awareness) and with this light we don't need to be scared of the dark (our fears). Shine the light on these fears that we imagine, build the courage to face them, understand them, embrace them, work through them and then watch them disappear. Over time, with your courage, you will build confidence – and that is the antidote for fear.

Failure led to LIGHT

Another fear that can slow us down is the fear of failure. Even when it comes to setting goals, people resist for fear of failure. If they don't set the goal, - they don't need to achieve it, and then there is no way for them to feel failure…very sad.

Do you know who invented the light bulb? Most people say it was Thomas Edison - and they would be partially correct. Thomas Edison was an inventor and patented many inventions. He did not invent the light bulb, but instead invented the first commercially practical incandescent light.

Now, Edison didn't just go into his lab and come out with a working light bulb. He had to work hours, days, and months to get it to work and keep working as a sustainable light source. He failed many times working to get it right. He experimented with different types of filaments that could sustain light for longer periods of time. Finally, he landed on a filament made of bamboo that came from Japan to make it work. When asked about all these failures, he is famous for saying, "I have not failed. I've just found 10,000 ways that won't work". What a brilliant perspective.

The Light Bulb Strategy

Brilliance in Action:

Exercise – Shine LIGHT on your Fears:

What fears may be holding you back from being brilliant?

On a piece of paper, write out these fears. What action can you take to face these fears, work through them and eliminate them?

The 60 Watt LIGHT Bulb – Limiting Beliefs

When you look at a standard incandescent light bulb, you see printed right on the bulb the wattage of the bulb - 60 watts. That is the limit of power that bulb can generate; - it is labelled with a limit. People can behave the same way and become bound by their own limiting beliefs. They make excuses like, "I'm not smart enough.", "I don't have time to do that." After hearing all this self-talk, they form barriers in themselves from reaching their true potential.

Again, it gets back to understanding and being more aware of yourself. Are there self-talk barriers you are telling yourself that may be holding you back? Are you making excuses? Do you believe in yourself?

Author Jack Canfield who is known for his *Chicken Soup for the Soul* series of books says in his book, *The Success Principles*, "It's now *your* responsibility to take charge of your own self-concept and your beliefs. You must choose to believe that you can do anything you set your mind to - anything at all – because, in fact, you can. It might help you to know that the latest brain research now indicates that with enough positive self-talk and positive visualization combined with the proper training, coaching, and practice, anyone can learn to do almost anything."

What would it take to get you to become a 100 watt light bulb? - A 1,000 watt light bulb? - A 5,000 watt light bulb?! Change the way you talk to yourself. Instead of saying "I don't have time to do that", - say "How can I find time to do that?" When you ask yourself a question, your brain goes to work to find the answer.

<u>**Brilliance in Action:**</u>

Exercise – The 60 Watt Light Bulb:

What limiting beliefs are holding you back?

What are you saying to yourself?

Write down these things that you are saying to yourself that may be holding you back.

Identify how this belief is holding you back. What feelings does it give you?

Change what you have written down by rewording it so that it gives you a positive statement or a positive question that your brain can work on.

What feelings does this new statement or question give you?

The Light Bulb Strategy

Mood LIGHTS – Our Attitude

We are all just big Mood LIGHTS. We can be happy, sad, angry, excited, positive, and negative; the list goes on and on. What kind of Mood Light do you give off most of the time? How does that behavior affect you and others around you? How do the behaviors given off by other people affect you?

When it comes to being truly successful, attitude is everything. We must be accountable for our attitudes and our actions. As Winston Churchill once said, "Attitude is a little thing that makes a big difference." And Zig Ziglar said, "Your Attitude, not your Aptitude, will determine your Altitude."

We get to decide how we behave and react to what life throws our way – good or bad. Our attitude is one thing that is totally in our control. We must be able to adapt and keep our attitude positive. Remember, it's not the mistakes we make, but how we react to those mistakes that counts. Do you blame others or do you take responsibility and take action to correct?

There has been a lot written about Emotional Intelligence (sometimes abbreviated as EI or EQ which stands for Emotional Quotient). This is very similar to the Intelligence Quotient or IQ. A very important part of building your base is having a good understanding of your emotional self; being aware of your emotions. You need to understand the impact they have on you and others. Management of your emotions is critical to your success in work and personal life. It is the foundation for building strong relationships.

You need to be in control of your emotions. You need to be in control of what you say to people and how you say it. Sometimes when we speak our mind without control we can hurt other people. When you get into an emotional situation, you are better to wait and think about what you are going to say. If required, give yourself a time-out. Go for a walk, have a coffee break or leave the office early.

Many people play the blame game. If things don't go their way, they are quick to blame other things, other people, and circumstances for their problems and issues, when what they should be doing is looking at themselves in the mirror and taking full responsibility.

People need to stop blaming, stop complaining and take action. They need to get out of their comfort zone where it is easy to blame and complain. Getting out of your comfort zone by breaking through the barriers that are holding you back is an important step to becoming brilliant.

Remember, your attitude is habit as well – driven by your thoughts. As James Allen writes in his classic book, *As a Man Thinketh*, "You are today where your thoughts have brought you; you will be tomorrow where your thoughts take you."

If you have a negative attitude, it will have a negative impact on the trajectory of your life. So what do you do? Change your attitude by changing your thoughts!

<u>Brilliance in Action:</u>

Exercise – Mood Lights: Evaluate your Attitude

How would you rate your attitude on the "Dimmer Switch" scale? Positive or Negative?

Do you have a positive attitude most of the time?

The Light Bulb Strategy

Do you look for the positive outcomes that come out of negative situations?

What can you do to change your attitude and be more positive?
What negative thoughts can you change to positive thoughts?

What will you now say to yourself that will give you a positive attitude?

The next step of *The Light Bulb Strategy* is to envision your light bulb in the future!

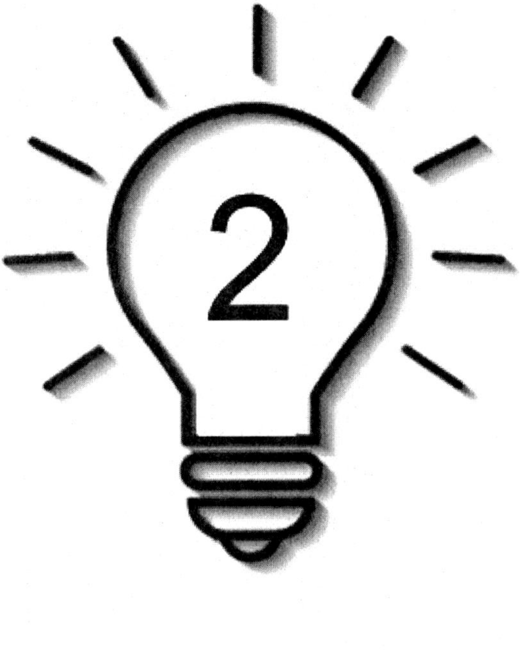
2

The Light Bulb Strategy Blueprint

1) Core Base
Who are you?
Values, Beliefs,
Experiences, Passions,
Habits, Attitude

2) Outer Casing Grooves
What do you want to do?
→ Define your Mission
→ Define your Vision
→ Start Defining Goals

The Light Bulb Strategy

*"Know what sparks the light in you.
Then use that light to illuminate the world."*
Oprah Winfrey

Step 2

ENVISION YOUR LIGHT BULB OF THE FUTURE
"The Future looks Brilliant."

It was about 10 minutes to 8:00 when I was driving my 12 year old son Nicholas to elementary school. We had an interesting conversation on the way to school - girl troubles. I offered my best advice I could as a father - that's my job. We pulled into the school parking lot. I have a saying that I use with my kids when I drop them off at school, put them on the school bus or say goodbye as they walk out the front door of the house - "Work Hard, Play Hard, Build your Base."

My son challenged me on this one day. "What do you mean - Build your Base?" He braced himself for the lecture that was quick to follow.

I explained, "You need to work and play to develop yourself every day, and elementary school is a big part of getting the basic learnings you require to help you grow and develop as a person. You learn to read, write, do math and interact with other people. As you get older this base education will help you move on to what you really want to do with your life. Like a rocket blasting into space to reach the stars, it needs a strong base foundation or launch pad to make it happen."
"Uh huh" was his response.

Robert Craig

Later, I asked my son what he is passionate about and what he wants to do when he gets older. "I want to be an actor or a game show host and if that doesn't work I will be a movie critic or a police officer." He has a dream that he is passionate about and a backup plan!

To support his passion, we got Nicholas a talent agent about a year and a half ago. Since then he has worked as an actor in movies and television. One of the movies he was in went to the Sundance and Cannes Film Festivals. He has made appearances on the Discovery Channel, PBS Kids and YTV. He looks to the future and wants to continue his passion for acting.

When our middle son Kevin was young he wanted to become an astronaut. Then one fateful day when the space shuttle didn't make it through re-entry, he reconsidered his career choice. Still loving technology, Kevin is pursuing his passion of computer game programming and design. He's working on developing a computer game that he plans to release and market in the future.

Our oldest son Matthew is a hockey fanatic. When he was young we were always at the rink early for practice. During the coldest wintery months when we thought we wouldn't be able to get him out of his warm bed – he would jump out of bed when we came to wake him. Other times he would come into our room and wake us up to ask if it was time for hockey. Today, Matthew is working to graduate with a diploma in Marketing and Advertising. He has a keen eye for detail and has designed some advertisements for his local newspaper. He even helped me with the design of my book cover. He is pursuing his passion by pursuing a career in Sports Marketing.

The second step of "The Light Bulb Strategy" is to envision your light bulb in the future by getting clear on WHAT you want to do with your life.

The Light Bulb Strategy

Get in the Groove, Not in a Rut

Our core is the platform that drives our behavior in what we want to do and why. And because our core is built by ourselves **only we can decide** what we want to do in our life - no one can choose it for us if we want to be truly happy.

On "The Light Bulb Strategy Blueprint", the grooves coming out of the base of the light bulb (the screw cap) represent WHAT you want to do with your life.

The grooves are a significant part of the light bulb. If you put a light bulb into a ceiling fixture with no grooves, what will happen? Right – it will fall out. The grooves are needed so the light bulb stays secure in the socket. This is very important, especially when life knocks you off course (and it will!). A strong base with rich grooves will help you stay in place and work through the challenges you encounter so you can achieve goals towards your vision and continue your journey towards your mission.

You need to determine what your rich grooves are and avoid getting into a rut. Some people just take each day as it comes. They get stuck in regular routines just to make it through the day. It's not that they aren't busy. Many people are just busy doing unimportant things; - they form habits (not always good ones) and get into a routine that will not allow them to grow. When you look at grooves at the base of their light bulb, they have become stuck in place.

Have you ever removed a light bulb from its socket and found it difficult to remove - like it has been rusted, corroded in place? That's the point I am making - you need to be constantly reviewing WHAT you want to do and change it up so you don't get stuck in a rut, get too comfortable and lose out on achieving your purpose in life.

On "The Light Bulb Strategy Blueprint" you see three grooves on the base of the light bulb. They represent your mission, your vision and your goals. Although in reality there is only one continuous groove on a light bulb (the screw cap) – the blueprint shows that they are all dependent on each other – they are intertwined! To achieve your mission – you need a vision, and to achieve your vision you will need goals.

So how do you ensure you get a strong base with rich grooves? Seek clarity.

The Clear LIGHT Bulb

A clear light bulb is fully transparent. It allows you to see all the details and inner workings that make it function. Whether you are defining your purpose (your mission – why you exist), articulating your vision of the future, or defining goals, you need to be crystal clear on what you want. When you write them down (and you do need to write them down) be clear and precise about what it is you want.

A clear light bulb will shine brighter than a frosted light bulb. When you are a frosted light bulb, - you lack clarity, direction, control, and you just go through life day by day, often unfulfilled.

When you have clarity, you have more control and can focus on what is important to you. You will be able to make better decisions and better choices.

So…let's get clear on what we want – by shining a light in our face - The Interrogation LIGHT!

The Light Bulb Strategy

The Interrogation LIGHT

The room was dark; only a chair and table sat in the centre of the room. The light swung down over the table held only from a lone wire hanging from the ceiling. There he sat, shaking his head.

"What do you mean you don't know?" I asked staring at him intently.

He looked up at me, squinting from the light in his eyes, "I don't know!"

"Sooner or later you're going to have to decide", I said. "I'm going to ask the question again, what do you want to do with your life?"

He sat there thinking, "I just need a little more time to figure it out."

That's the reality a lot of people experience today, they don't know WHAT they really want to do.

People wonder why they aren't getting ahead in life. They hope that one day success will magically find them and then they will have all the freedom and money to do whatever they want when they want. That is not going to happen without a plan.

As Jim Rohn said, "If you don't design your own life plan, chances are you'll fall into someone else's plan. And guess what they have planned for you? Not much."

You need to shine the Interrogation LIGHT in your face and get serious about what you want to do with your life so that you can grow and as a result – become brilliant.

Are you doing what you want to do with your life? Do you know what it is you want to do? Do you know what you are passionate about? What brings you Joy?

Brilliance in Action:

Exercise - The Interrogation Light:

Have someone sit (or stand) facing you. Have them ask you, "What do you want to do with your life?" This can be personal or professional things. When you answer, have them ask the question again immediately, "What do you want to do with your life?" repeat this until you can't answer any more. Then capture by writing down what you said. Look at your list. How do the items on your list make you feel? Surprised? Excited? From this list you should be able to shed some light on what you are passionate about. This is the key to help you identify your potential goals, vision and mission.

You can download "The Interrogation Light" form from my website at www.TheLightBulbStrategy.com

The Interrogation Light

What do you want to do?

_____
_____
_____
_____
_____
_____
_____
_____
_____
_____
_____
_____
_____

The Light Bulb Strategy

The Search LIGHT

Many people are still searching for what they want to do with their life; they are unsure. They could spend the majority of their life doing work they don't truly enjoy. To be truly happy, you need to find your passion - something that will give you meaning and purpose. You need to take time to think; look to the future and envision what you truly want to do to grow as a person and feel fulfilled.

The power of the mind is incredible. You need to look into the future and visualize what you want. To search for it! How do you discover what you want? How do you determine your purpose and meaning? You need to ask yourself great questions – "Brilliant Questions". If you ask "Brilliant Questions", you can get brilliant answers.

As Gary Keller says in his book *The One Thing*, "One of the most empowering moments in my life came when I realized that life is a question and how we live it is our answer. How we phrase the questions we ask ourselves determines the answers that eventually become our life."

Here are some brilliant questions you can ask yourself to help you get started.

Brilliance in Action:

Exercise: Search Light Questions

How do you like to spend your time?

What do you love to do?

What hobbies do you enjoy?

The Light Bulb Strategy

Who do you love spending time with?

Where do you like to spend your time?

If you were given all the money you wanted, what would you do with it?

How would you spend your time?

What comes easy to you while others find it difficult to do?

What did you like to do when you were a child?

It will take some time to work through this – you need to give it a lot of thought. Write down your thoughts on paper. By writing your ideas down you actually get a sense of relief because you no longer have all your ideas bouncing around in your head.

Look at the answers you have written down. Do you see any themes coming out of what you have written? Are you excited about what you see on the page? Is there something in particular that stands out? Do you see things that you are passionate about?

Don't be an Artificial LIGHT

"You have to be unique, and different and shine in your own way." - Lady Gaga

Artificial light is light that simulates natural light. However, artificial light is fake, contrived and imitated. When it comes to doing what you want to do and being what you want to be, only you can truly decide. You need to be real with yourself. Don't be an artificial light – an imitation of someone else; being someone that someone else has in mind for you. Be genuine, be one of a kind, be you, be brilliant!

"Be yourself, everyone else is already taken." - Oscar Wilde

Natural LIGHT

To be successful, you should focus on what you are naturally good at (your strengths) and what you enjoy doing (your passion). When you find your WHAT and it connects with your strengths and passion, you will be more purposeful, more dedicated, more brilliant!

For example, if you love photography and you're good at it, perhaps you could become a professional photographer. Or perhaps you enjoy working with numbers and have a knack for mathematics; maybe you should consider accounting, banking or investment consulting.

Brilliance in Action:

Exercise: Natural Light Questions

What strengths do you have?

What do you do that you find easy while others find difficult?

What passions do you have?

What activities are you good at and are passionate about? Make a list of these activities.

Could you make money from these activities?

The Light Bulb Strategy

Dancing into the LIGHT

Our time here on earth is limited. We need to live life to the fullest, having no regrets! Another technique I learned to get perspective on what is important to you is to fast forward and visualize the end of your life; to see yourself in your final days on earth. It sounds very morbid and people don't like to do it. They don't like to think about the end of their lives, but take some time to think about it, to visualize it.

Ask yourself as you look to the end - What are your surroundings? Who is with you? Your spouse, your children, your grandchildren, your friends? What are they saying to you? What are they saying to each other about you? Listen to their conversations - do you like what they are saying? Does it give you comfort? What would you want to hear them say that would give you comfort?

Let me share with you my experience. I visualize my wife saying to me in my final hours...

"We've had such a great life together. I am so proud of you! You have been my best friend and have always been there for me. Our kids have grown and developed into fine adults. Their kids are growing; - their whole lives ahead of them. What an example you have provided for them - a family legacy that they will cherish and pass down to the next generation. You have made such a great contribution in helping others develop and grow themselves through your teachings. Your continuous learning mindset is contagious."

Then I go through and visualize the conversation with my kids, grandchildren, friends and colleagues. What do I want them to be saying to me? Capture and write down what you want them to be saying to you. Those words they say - they are your mission; the reason you exist. You were a great Husband, Father and Teacher. My "Mission of Brilliance" is to be a great family man (father, husband, brother and son) and to be a great teacher.

When I get to the end of my life and shut my eyes for the last time, I will know in my heart that I have accomplished my Life Missions. I will accept going into the light and dance my way in....

Candle LIGHT

If you find visualizing the end of your life to be too difficult, another technique that is used by personal development trainers is to think ahead to a milestone birthday later in your life, say your 90th birthday party.

As this birthday is a significant milestone, visualize the party that has been arranged for your celebration. Visualize your surroundings – where is the party taking place? It could be taking place in a banquet hall, in a restaurant, in a backyard on a sunny day. What color are the balloons? What kind of food is being served? Who is there? What speeches or toasts are being made? What are they saying? What do you want them to be saying about you?

Visualize your birthday cake with all those candles! The candle light is significant – each candle representing a year of your life. How do you want to have spent those years?

The Light Bulb Strategy

<u>Brilliance in Action:</u>

Exercise – Find your "Mission of Brilliance"

Take some quiet time to do this exercise.

Visualize your 90th birthday party or visualize the end of your life (or do both – as each will reveal similar and different feelings).

What do you want people to be saying about you?

Capture and write down what you want them to say. These words you write down will help you find your Mission (purpose) in life.

LIGHT up your Vision

Once you have established your overall purpose in life, why you exist – Your "Mission of Brilliance", then you can look to craft your Vision. Your Vision is about looking into the future and seeing the life you want to have - seeing a future that is absolutely brilliant to you.

How far into the future do you look? That's up to you; it's your vision. The great thing about your vision is that you can't be wrong (as long as you are true to yourself and not an artificial light). Depending on the scope and complexity of your vision it could be 1 year, 5 years or 10 years.

As I explained earlier in the chapter, we must use "Clear Light Bulb" thinking. You need to spend the time to visualize where you want to be in the future with absolute clarity. Get as detailed as possible in seeing your vision with your mind's eye. The clearer you are about where you want to go the easier it will be to determine how to get there. And yes – seeing your journey along the way is an important part of defining your vision. After all it's all about living the life **you** want! To be **your** best self – to be brilliant!

When working on your vision think big, don't set limits on yourself – No "60 Watt Light Bulbs" here! Work through these questions below as they will help you light your vision in the different areas of your life – career/job, personal time, health, relationships, community service, spirituality and finances.

<u>**Brilliance in Action:**</u>

Exercise: Light up your Vision

Close your eyes and think to your future – what do you want to be doing?

Where do you want to be?

Who do you want to be with?

How do you want to spend your free time?

How do you envision your health?

How would you describe your perfect job, your perfect career?

Capture all your thoughts – write them down and put together a vision statement of your ideal future.

You should review your vision statement regularly – it should help to keep you motivated and focused.

The Light Bulb Strategy

The Goal LIGHT

Once you have captured your mission and your vision for the future, you can start to think about setting goals. Goals give you something to aim for; they also give you purpose.

When you set goals, you want to ensure that WHAT you are going to do is the right things. Metaphorically, you don't want to spend your time climbing the wrong mountain, or putting your ladder up against the wrong wall. You want to ensure you are working to be brilliant and light up the right space! Your goals should connect and support your vision and mission.

There really is an art and science to writing goals. The key word here is "writing" goals. You need to write them down! It's about having clarity (Clear Light Bulb) and when you have clarity your brain goes to work to make it happen.

There are countless books and articles on how to go about writing goals. One method that is very well known uses the acronym "SMART". Each letter is a reminder for how we can write effective goals. SMART goals are **S**pecific, **M**easurable, **A**ttainable, **R**elevant, and **T**imely.

We need to ensure our goal is very Specific - so specific that we could give the goal to another person and they would know clearly what it is they need to do to accomplish it. The goal needs to define what we are going to do, why we are doing it and how we are going to do it.

We also need to ensure our goal is Measurable. Any manager will tell you that you can't improve something that you can't measure. Measurement lets you know clearly whether you have attained the goal or not. The answer will be black and white – yes or no. It is your evidence of success. All of your inputs lead to this output.

We need to ensure the goal is Attainable. You want the goal to stretch you but you don't want it to be impossible to achieve. Impossible goals will just demotivate you and stop you once you encounter your first challenge.

We need to ensure the goal is Relevant. That is, the goal should be working towards your vision and your mission. Again, you want to be brilliant by lighting up the right space!

Lastly, we need to ensure the goal is Timely. We need to set a boundary of time – a deadline to accomplish the goal. This gives us a sense of urgency that will help us maximize our limited resource of time.

Your Name in LIGHTS

A great way to accomplish your big goals for the year is to declare to the world that you have completed them! That is, look to the end of the year and write out your big goals as if you have already done them. I recommend you choose three big goals for the year – "Big Brilliant Goals" - that when you accomplish them will have the greatest positive impact on your life.

I think we have all seen theatres with large billboard type marquee signs surrounded by lights telling you what performance is being featured. In this case, we are featuring your performance for the year and letting the world know what great things you have done.

Let's say one of my big goals for the year was to lose 20 pounds. I could put on the marquee sign: "Lost 20 pounds and is full of energy". It is a high level declaration of the goal completed. Of course, I will have written out the goal using the SMART criteria as well – That is: "By December 31, I will have

The Light Bulb Strategy

lost at least 20 pounds by going to the gym 3 times a week and drinking 6 glasses of water daily."

"Your Name in Lights" is a great tool to use to keep your big goals front and center. You could print it out and keep it on your fridge, your bathroom mirror – anywhere you want so that it reminds you of your big three "Big Brilliant Goals" for the year.

<u>*Brilliance in Action:*</u>

What would you like your marquee sign to say, if you wanted to tell the world what three "Big Brilliant Goals" you will have accomplished this year?

Use the "Your Name in Lights" form and fill out what you would like to declare you will have done by the end of the year. I have included my marquee sign on the next page.

Throughout the different steps of "The Light Bulb Strategy", you will encounter many opportunities to set other goals for achievement in the various areas of your life. As you do so, use the SMART criteria to ensure your goals are effective.

In the next step, you will power up your light bulb!

What a Year!

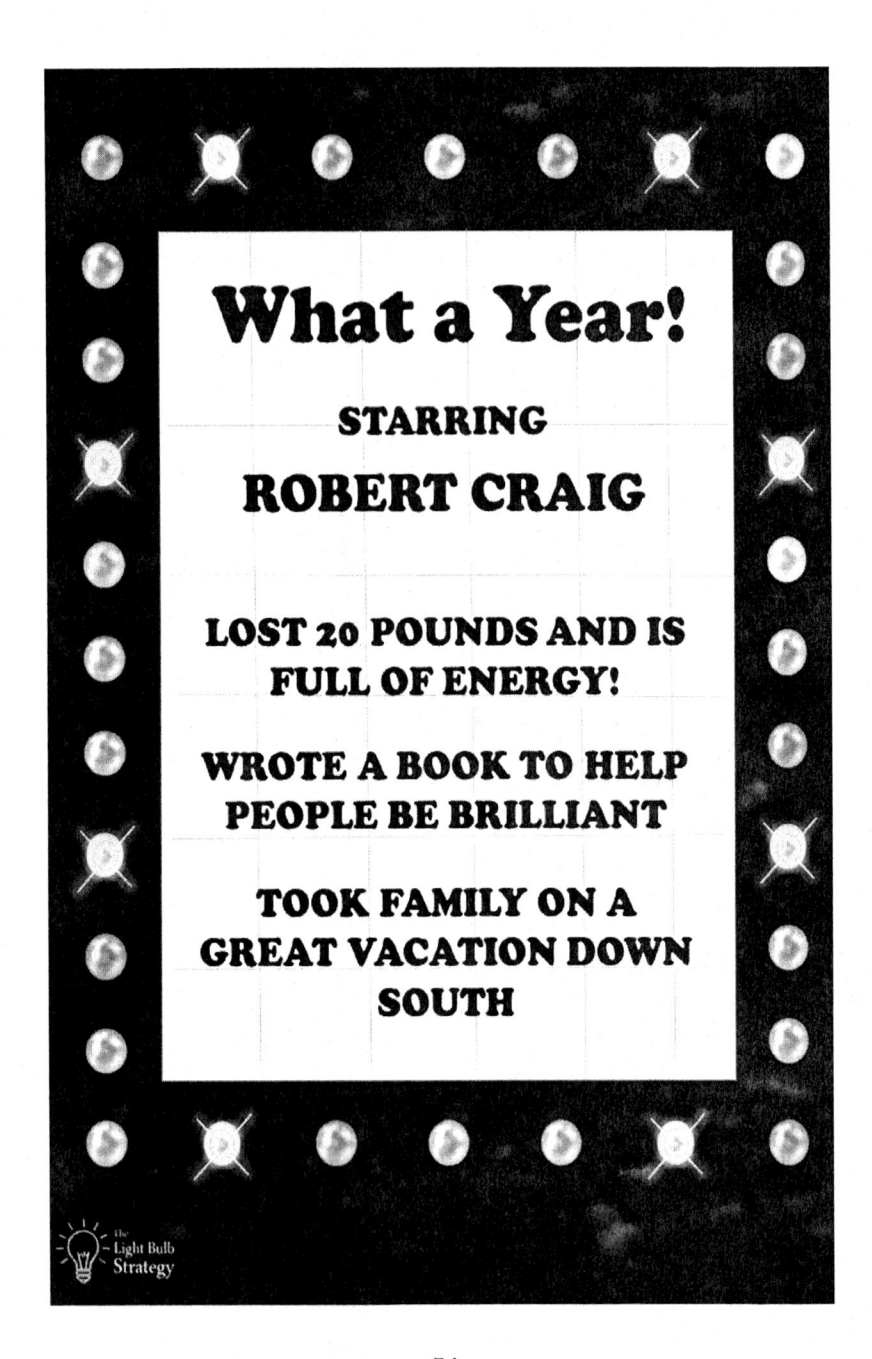

STARRING
ROBERT CRAIG

LOST 20 POUNDS AND IS FULL OF ENERGY!

WROTE A BOOK TO HELP PEOPLE BE BRILLIANT

TOOK FAMILY ON A GREAT VACATION DOWN SOUTH

the Light Bulb Strategy

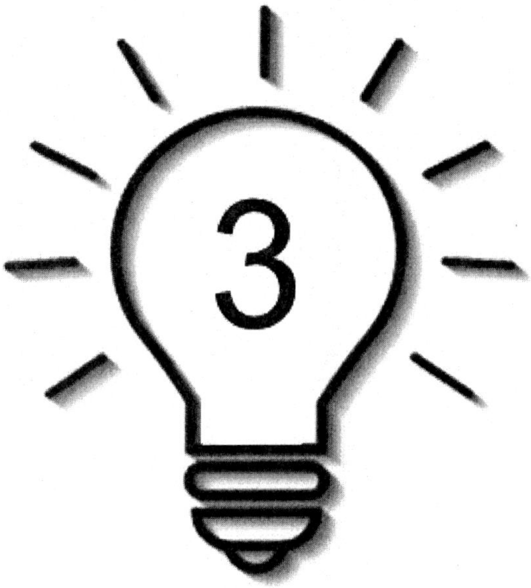
3

The Light Bulb Strategy Blueprint

1) Core Base
Who are you?
Values, Beliefs,
Experiences, Passions,
Habits, Attitude

2) Outer Casing Grooves
What do you want to do?
→ Define your Mission
→ Define your Vision
→ Start Defining Goals

3) Contact Point
What are your Sources of Energy?
Why Power
Power Drivers:
Health, Relationships, Finances

The
Light Bulb
Strategy

"Energy and Persistence conquer all things."
Benjamin Franklin

Step 3

POWER-UP YOUR LIGHT BULB

"Get the Energy you need to be Brilliant."

You have done a lot of work to define WHAT it is you want to do with your life; you have defined your mission and crafted your vision for the future. You also received a quick primer on how to create effective goals using the SMART criteria which we will soon put into practice.

Once you have decided WHAT you want to do, you need to challenge yourself to determine WHY you want to do it. This is your gut check and you must check it frequently to ensure that your WHY is aligned with your WHAT. Knowing WHAT you want to do satisfies the left side of your brain, where logic and reasoning reside. Knowing WHY you want to do it satisfies the need from the right side of your brain, your feelings and beliefs.

The third step of "The Light Bulb Strategy" is to power up your light bulb by getting clear on WHY you want to do what you want to do, and having the resources to sustain it.

You need to understand your motivation; your purpose for what you want to do. Again, if you're not sure WHY you want to do something or your reasons are weak, - you will stop doing your WHAT when things go off course.

On "The Light Bulb Strategy Blueprint", your WHY is represented on the light bulb as the contact tip. - It is the point where the light bulb receives its power; - in this case - WHY power! This is what drives you, motivates you, and keeps you going when faced with obstacles and challenges.

For example, say you have determined that you want to become a lawyer. You need to list out your reasons WHY you want to be a lawyer. Are you satisfying your own passion here or are you satisfying the needs of another person?

So many times people go into things because of expectations from other people. Be sure the reasons WHY you want to do something are your reasons; -   only you can answer the question of what is your WHY.

WHY Power in Action

In his great book, *The Compound Effect*, author Darren Hardy provides an excellent example of how the WHY principle can be applied. He talks about putting a plank of wood on the ground (10 inches wide; 30 feet in length) and asks, "If you walk the length of the plank, I'll give you twenty dollars"; would you do it? Of course, it's an easy twenty bucks." Then he goes on to say, "But what if I took that same plank and made a roof-top 'bridge' between two 100-storey buildings? That same twenty dollars for walking the thirty-foot plank no longer looks desirable or even possible, does it? You'd look at me and say, 'Not on your life.' However, if your child was on the opposite building, and the building was on fire, would you walk the length of the plank to save him? Without question and immediately – you'd do it, twenty dollars or not." That is the power of knowing your WHY!

The Light Bulb Strategy

Check Your Wiring!

To power our light bulb we need our WHY power connector to receive a sustainable power source. The main WHY power is like the main breaker of an electrical panel in a house. From the main breaker there are other breaker switches that control power to many different things. On "The Light Bulb Strategy Blueprint", I call these *Power Drivers*. They feed into the main WHY power line and can either add (enablers) or detract (disablers) from the power feeding your light bulb. These *Power Drivers* have a significant impact on how brilliantly you can get your light bulb to shine.

Heart LIGHT – Your Main Source of Power

The main *Power Driver* is your health – Your Heart Light! This is something you need to protect and manage well. You need to see your doctor on a regular basis, get proper exercise, sleep well and maintain a proper diet. These are all key *Power Drivers!* Health is your main breaker switch that controls how brilliantly your light bulb can shine. Your health habits are critical to sustaining your brilliance!

The Bike LIGHT – Exercising Right

How would you rate your habits as they relate to exercise? If you have positive exercise habits - that is you exercise regularly, then your dimmer switch would be relatively high. If you don't exercise at all, then the dimmer switch would be low. This reduces the power that can get to your light bulb. If your dimmer switch continues to stay low, in the long term you will have problems being able to sustain your brilliant light. Work to exercise daily and move your body. You should schedule time in your calendar for exercise. And always consult with your doctor to determine the right type and amount of exercise for you.

<u>**Brilliance in Action:**</u>

Define your current habits as they relate to exercise – write them down.

What are (will become) your "Habits of Brilliance" for exercising?

Using the SMART criteria, what goal will you set to ensure you are exercising right?

The Night LIGHT – Sleeping Right

One of the most important things you can do is get a good night's sleep. We need sleep to rejuvenate our bodies. Sleep is when our bodies heal.

If you don't sleep well your dimmer switch will be low – which truly affects how you function in the world. If you sleep well and

The Light Bulb Strategy

wake up full of energy then your dimmer switch is high and provides the energy you need to achieve peak performance.

I've had trouble sleeping in the past. I later discovered I had minor sleep apnea – I would stop breathing when I slept. I would also snore, which also affected my wife's sleep.

I went to a sleep clinic – the first time to assess my sleep. I arrived at the clinic in the evening, sat in the waiting room with other patients – all in our pajamas. It's been awhile since I have been to a pajama party – awkward! They wired me up with all kinds of sensors and walked me to my bedroom. They monitored me while I slept. They discovered my sleep apnea and also said that I kick in my sleep.

On my second sleep clinic visit they wired me up the same way but then provided me with a CPAP machine. A CPAP is a machine that comes with a mask that provides air pressure flow into your nostrils while you sleep. The next morning I woke and I recalled doing something I had not done in a long time – dream.

I use a CPAP machine all the time now. I sleep better; my wife sleeps better because I no longer snore. One side effect of my CPAP is that I occasionally get sore ribs. Sore ribs, you're asking? Sometimes when I crawl into bed I will just lie there – then I may start dozing off. That's when it happens; I get an elbow to the ribs from my wife; "You're snoring – put your mask on!"

The other thing I use when I sleep is a mouth guard. I grind my teeth when I sleep. My dentist noticed I was cracking my teeth because of the extreme pressure I was putting on them while I slept. The mouth guard helps to reduce the pressure and impact on my teeth and gums.

So when I go to bed, I have my mask and my mouth guard. I look like a fighter pilot about to step into the boxing ring! It's a small price to pay in order to sleep right.

If you sleep well then congratulations are in order; - you have been given a true gift. If you don't sleep well, get help to find out why. Read about sleep, learn about sleep. And get the professional help you need to get a good-night's sleep.

<u>Brilliance in Action:</u>

Define your current habits as they relate to sleep – write them down.

What are (will become) your "Habits of Brilliance" for sleeping right?

Using the SMART criteria, what goal will you set to ensure you are getting a good night sleep?

The Fridge LIGHT – Eating Right

If you have positive diet habits and eat well then your dimmer switch will be high providing superior energy to your light bulb. If you have a constant diet of fast food, sugary food, your dimmer switch will be low - again the long term effects of a bad diet could affect your ability to make your light bulb shine. If the bad diet habits continue, it could burn out your light bulb for good!

<u>Brilliance in Action:</u>

Define your current habits as they relate to eating right – write them down.

What are (will become) your "Habits of Brilliance" for eating right?

Using the SMART criteria, what goal will you set to ensure you are eating right and getting the proper nutrition you need?

Switch-Off!

That's right – Switch-Off! Beyond getting enough sleep, it is so important that we take time off to relax and re-energize our power. I find it surprising the number of people who don't take all their vacation - like it is some sort of badge of honor. "The business can't survive without me" – That is 60 watt light bulb thinking – it's a limiting belief!

Your body, mind and soul need time to rejuvenate. You need to recharge your batteries – your power supply. When your power supply is recharged you will be able to make better decisions and be more creative. In fact, when your mind is able to relax you may come up with some of your best ideas. I know I have!

Later in the book we will talk about managing your calendar. One of the most important things you need to do is schedule time off from your busy schedule. You need to find some time and Switch -Off!

<u>Brilliance in Action:</u>

Define your current habits as they relate to taking time off – write them down.

What are (will become) your "Habits of Brilliance" for taking time off – to Switch -Off?

Using the SMART criteria, what goal will you set to ensure you are taking time off to recharge your energy?

LIGHT Connections - Relationships

The next *Power Driver* is so important. It can give us energy or take it away. And that is our relationships with others. To have our light bulb shine brilliantly, we need to build positive relationships. As part of building a strong base, positive relationships are the foundation for being successful.

How do we build and sustain great relationships? It all starts with trust – the foundation for brilliant relationships. As author Steven R. Covey wrote, "Trust is the glue of life. It's the most essential ingredient in effective communication and the foundational principle that holds all relationships together."

Whether it is a personal relationship with your significant other, a parent or a child, or a business relationship with a colleague, customer, boss or subordinate, trust is king.

Trust is the basis for brilliance. Without trust, the relationship suffers. Trust needs time to grow and once it is established it can be one of your greatest assets. An asset which you must protect. As the saying goes, "Trust takes years to build, seconds to break and forever to repair."

Relationships are precious, especially with our significant other...

The Light Bulb Strategy

Romantic LIGHTING

The lights were dimmed down low, soft music playing in the background. The fine dining restaurant was particularly busy that night, but we didn't really notice. We were lost in each other's eyes. We sat at a table sitting beside each other, not across from each other like a typical dining table. There was a beautiful fireplace that burned warmly removing the dampness on that cool fall evening. The candle on the table provided extra light so we could see our meals and more importantly each other. We were lost in our little part of the universe.

It was time. Time to walk out on the skinny branch, take a risk and ask the question that would change the trajectory of our lives. I got down on one knee, opened my carefully concealed ring box and said, "Andrée, will you marry me?"

Tears started to flow (her and me!) as she responded, "Yes Rob, I will marry you", and we embraced each other. The next thing we heard was the sound of applause from our neighboring tables, "Congratulations!"

It wasn't long after that we got married, had children and got caught up in the day-to-day craziness that comes with raising a family. But during the craziness, we always try to take the time to work on building our relationship.

"A relationship is like a house. When a light bulb burns out you do not go and buy a new house, you fix the light bulb." - Source Unknown.

Communication is so important. On the weekend we enjoy morning coffee together and calibrate on the upcoming activities for the week. We discuss family matters, financial matters and share our victories and defeats from the week. Of course we connect during the week and make any necessary course corrections.

There is a trap that many couples fall into after marriage. That is they think because they committed to each other and got married they don't need to try as hard on the relationship as when they were "courting". They become complacent in their relationship and take each other for granted. You need to keep that courting mentality alive! What can you do to woo your significant other? Plan a surprise date night, write a secret note, or give an unexpected gift for something they have accomplished or just to say Thank-you.

One of my wife's big goals was to get her real estate license – to follow her passion. She worked incredibly hard to study as she prepared for her exams. On her final exam she scored 99% - incredible! What an accomplishment! She was in our home office when I heard her cry out with joy when she saw her score results on-line. I came into the office and she was dancing in her chair. She showed me her score and I gave her a big hug. Then I handed her a little gift box. Inside was a small charm in the shape of a house for her Pandora bracelet. She was so surprised and her eyes filled with tears. It's sometimes just the littlest things that can make such a big difference to keep our relationships strong.

Spending time together is what it's all about. We schedule date nights to go out on the town. We schedule vacations every few years – just for the two of us - to reconnect. Of course we felt guilty leaving the kids behind with their grandparents, but it was important that we got our alone time.

One very memorable trip was the time we went to Las Vegas. There, we knocked off an item on our bucket list – we renewed our wedding vows with Elvis! That's right – The King! We've

The Light Bulb Strategy

also journeyed on a cruise through the Caribbean and enjoyed an all-inclusive in the Mayan Rivera. And then there are the romantic week-ends away as well.

Of course, we have had many family vacations with the kids. It's important that we build great memories with our kids – our Mini Lights!

Mini-LIGHTS – Our Kids

Our family is at the top of the priority list for my wife and me. My boys are my inspiration and keep me striving to be a better father. They give me lots of energy and also consume a lot of energy, but that's just fine. Raising great kids is part of my mission.

My wife and I have had so much fun watching them grow. Two of our boys are now bigger than me! The other one is not far behind.

Being a parent is such a huge responsibility. Our influence helps to shape their lives as they journey to become adults. We set the example that they see every day through their eyes. They are always watching to see how we act, react and behave. We need to teach them strong values, but more importantly we need to live to those values.

We need to allow them to make mistakes so they can learn from them. We need to let them try different things so they can discover what their own passions are. They need to be able to "Build their Base". That is to build a strong, secure base which will give them confidence and a sense of well-being.

Communication with our kids is vital as well. We need to spend time and listen to them, understand them. To listen to their victories and understand what concerns they have about the world they live in.

Our kids are our future. We need to teach them strong values, share family traditions and love them unconditionally. We need to listen to them, talk to them, educate them, be present for them and watch them become brilliant.

Brilliance in Action:

Define your current habits as they relate to building and maintaining strong relationships – write them down.

What are (will become) your "Habits of Brilliance" for building and maintaining strong relationships with the most important people in your life?

Using the SMART criteria, what goal will you set to ensure you are building and maintaining these strong relationships?

Attracted to the LIGHT

One thing that seems to happen when you start living your life with purpose is that people and things become attracted to your light. People and resources seem to appear from nowhere.

The Light Bulb Strategy

They appear and can help you succeed because you have consciously (and unconsciously) been looking for them. When you are clear what you want your brain goes to work to make it a reality.

The Law of Attraction – as Wikipedia defines it: name given to the term that "like attracts like" and that by focusing on positive or negative thoughts, one can bring about positive or negative results. This belief is based upon the idea that people and their thoughts are both made from "pure energy", and the belief that like energy attracts like energy.

"When you rise in the morning, give thanks for the light, for your life, for your strength. Give thanks for your food and the joy of living. If you see no reason to give thanks, the fault lies in yourself." - Tecumseh

In order to get more of what you want in life you need to give it first. You want more love? Be more loving. If you want more compassion, – be more compassionate. If you want more support, – be more supportive.

If you want more abundance in your life, you must think about abundance all around you. One way to increase your feelings of abundance is through gratitude. That is, being thankful for what you have in your life instead of what you don't have. It's about awareness of what you have that brings you joy. It can be very simple things that you are grateful for – a hot meal that was delicious, a beautiful sunset, a colorful flower that popped in your garden or a hug from your child. By thinking about what you have and being thankful for it you actually become happier, which gives you more energy.

Napoleon Hill writes, "Whatever the mind can conceive and believe, it can achieve."

Brilliance in Action:

Exercise – *"Attracted to the Light"*

What are you thankful for? Think about 2-3 things daily – write them down.

One powerful way to get more energy from gratitude is to start a "Gratitude Journal". Write in your journal 2-3 things you are thankful for.

The Banker's LIGHT

Another *Power Driver* is money. Money is an important resource to have as an enabler for doing what we want to do. How we think about and manage money can have a huge impact on our brilliance. It's all about mindset.

When it comes to money, "The Law of Attraction" comes into play again. If we always focus on not having money, – that is what our brain will focus on - not having money. However, if we think and focus on there being an abundance of money out there (and we believe we deserve to have more money), our brains will work to make that happen.

The Light Bulb Strategy

I'm not a banker, a broker or a financial advisor, but I do know quite a bit about financial management. In my current position I work with the major banks on programs to provide our franchisees with financing.

My university degree is in Economics. As part of my studies, I completed many accounting courses. One of the best things you can do is understand some basic accounting. Learning how financial statements work and the types of transactions that get recorded as journal entries to make those financial statements.

The basic financial concepts are the same for business and personal finance. You want to make more money than you spend so you have a positive cash flow. As they say, "cash is king!" You need to understand the concepts of assets (things you own that have value) and liabilities (amounts you owe). The difference between assets and liabilities is your equity or net worth.

Take the time to learn about financial management. This knowledge is useful for business and for personal use. If financial management is not your strength, work with a financial advisor or an accountant to help you navigate and plan your finances.

One of the most important things you can do is plan for your financial future. Yes, you need to take care of today, but you need to look to the future and determine how much money you will need to retire. Again, work a financial advisor or an accountant to help you figure this out.

My wife and I have many types of investments for our retirement. One method for building wealth that we like is real estate investing. We have spent a lot of time reading and attending conferences about real estate investing. At the time of writing, we own four houses and are working to invest in more.

Investing in real estate is more hands on than just investing in a stock or mutual fund. But, what's great about real estate is that you don't need to own the property outright to make an income from it. If you want to get dividend from a stock, you need to hold the whole stock share. You can have a mortgage on the property, but still get the full income potential if you rent it out. And although a mortgage is a form of debt, it is good debt because you have an asset that can grow and make you more money. Bad debt is debt that accumulates because of consumption; - buying meals on credit, or other consumer goods like clothing or electronics.

My wife and I have learned that you can make money four ways with an investment real estate property. First, when you buy a property (that needs some work) and you fix it up properly, you could increase its value. This is called forced appreciation. Hopefully after you are done with your renovations, the value of the home is now worth more than the cost of the house plus the renovations completed.

A second way you could make money from real estate investing is simple market appreciation. Over time the value of your home should appreciate in the marketplace. You should

The Light Bulb Strategy

do some homework to understand what the rates of market appreciation are for the area you are looking to invest.

The third way you could make money is by renting out the property. Again, you need to do your homework on finding and screening for good tenants. When tenants pay their rent, these payments should help you pay down your mortgage monthly.

The fourth way you could make money is from positive cash flow. Renting out the property so it covers all your carrying costs for the property (mortgage, city taxes, insurance and maintenance) and then having additional money left over at the end of each month. This can become much valued residual income that can come in month after month after month!

Purchasing homes is expensive and you don't want to make mistakes. Again, do a lot of reading and studying on the subject. Consult with professionals and mentors to help you avoid pitfalls. Work with experts, – if an area does not fall within your area of knowledge.

One thing I learned is not to try and do too much of the work yourself. You need to get people to help you (Blue Lights – which I talk about in Chapter 4) such as a handyman or painter. Look to invest in professional trades-people to do plumbing and electrical work; you need to ensure these things are done right and to proper city codes.

The key to managing finances is being organized. Being organized saves you time and money. I have a filing system that works pretty well. I keep a three ring binder for each calendar year's finances. In each binder I have a divider for my bank documents - bank statements, mortgage statements and credit cards. I have separate tabs for each of my utilities and also keep tabs for city tax bills and annual insurance renewals.

I have a special folder for unpaid bills that I keep beside my desk (even though most of my bills are paid by automatic withdrawal). After the bill is paid, I file it away in the binder. I keep receipts in a mini accordion file by month for each year. If I ever need to go back to find a receipt (to do a product return), I will be able to find it quickly.

I know my system is a bit "old school" – why not keep all your bills documents filed electronically? That is your choice, but we must remember that paper is still considered a form of technology – I still like to handle a paper document – but that's just me.

I highly recommend you develop a budget for your personal finances so that you can plan for income and expenses. Pay yourself first by allocating money to savings and retirement investments. Save for your child's education. When budgeting, separate out fixed monthly expenses such as your mortgage, car payments, insurance. Then determine a budget for your variable expenses. Variable expenses are exactly as described – they vary each month such as groceries, utilities, eating out, buying clothes. Then it is very important that you track your spending so you can see how you are progressing and whether you need to cut spending in certain areas.

One of the most important things you can do is build your credit score. Ensuring you pay your bills on time is one way to build your credit score over time. You will want to have an excellent credit rating as this will be the foundation for being granted further credit in the future. You will need this to be able to purchase growth assets in the future. It is a good idea to pull your own credit report at least annually from a credit institution so that you can monitor activity on your report.

Brilliance in Action:

Exercise – "The Bankers Light"

Define your current habits as they relate to your finances – write them down.

What are (will become) your "Habits of Brilliance" for your finances?

Using the SMART criteria, what goal will you set to improve your finances?

The next step is to determine HOW you are going to do what you want to do...

4

The Light Bulb Strategy Blueprint

4) Support Stem
How do you do what you want to do?
Create your Plan
Get the Support you need

1) Core Base
Who are you?
Values, Beliefs, Experiences, Passions, Habits, Attitude

2) Outer Casing Grooves
What do you want to do?
- Define your Mission
- Define your Vision
- Start Defining Goals

3) Contact Point
What are your Sources of Energy?
Why Power
Power Drivers:
Health, Relationships, Finances

The Light Bulb Strategy

"Efficiency is doing things right; effectiveness is doing the right things."
                                                            Peter Drucker

Step 4

BUILD YOURSELF A BETTER LIGHT BULB
"Go from Bright to Brilliant."

Once you know WHO you are, WHAT you want to do, WHY you want to do it (and have sustainable energy resources to do it), then the next part of "The Light Bulb Strategy" is determining HOW you are going to do it. This is where you start building structure upon your base.

The fourth step of "The Light Bulb Strategy" is to build yourself a better light bulb by determining HOW you're going to do WHAT you want to do in the most effective way with limited resources.

On "The Light Bulb Strategy Blueprint", the HOW is represented by the support stem that comes up from the base of the light bulb. This is where you continue your plan on HOW you are going to achieve your vision by accomplishing your goals.

The High Efficiency LIGHT Bulb

The Incandescent light bulb is on its way out - It is being left behind and replaced by high efficiency light bulbs such as compact fluorescent and LED's.

We must look at ourselves the same way – are you being left behind? What are you doing to improve your skills? To do things better and more efficiently? To provide greater value to other people, your company or your community? We must always be looking for ways to improve our skills and productivity that will help us achieve our goals. We need to learn more and, in doing so, - reinvent ourselves.

So what's an efficient and effective way to learn and grow? Find some "Guiding Lights"!

Guiding LIGHTS – Help Show you the Way

Coaches, teachers and mentors are filled with experience and knowledge. They serve you as a Guiding Light and are a resource that you must tap into to be successful.

Our time is limited. We can't spend our precious time trying to find our way on our own. Why not learn from other people who have been there and discovered what works and what doesn't? They can warn us of the pitfalls to avoid and reveal shortcuts to success.

The Light Bulb Strategy

I want to share a great story that John Maxwell has in his book, *The 15 Invaluable Laws of Growth*. "There's a well-known story of an expert who is called by a company to look at their manufacturing system. It had broken down and everything was at a standstill. When the expert arrived, he carried nothing but a black bag.

Silently he walked around the equipment for a few minutes and then stopped. As he focused on one specific area of the equipment, he pulled a small hammer out of his bag and he tapped it gently. Suddenly everything began running again, and he quietly left.

The next day he sent a bill that made the manager go ballistic. It was for $1,000! Quickly the manger e-mailed the expert and wrote, "I will not pay this outrageous bill without it being itemized and explained." Soon he received an invoice with the following words:

For the tapping on the equipment with hammer - $1
For knowing where to tap - $999

That is the value of wisdom! Mentors with wisdom often show us where to tap."

I have many coaches and mentors in my life. I have a mentor at work to provide me council on my career path. I have a mentor who advises me on goal setting and execution. I have a coach to help me write who was an incredible resource as I wrote this book. I have a few coaches who are teaching my wife and me about real estate investing. We joined an organization dedicated to educating people about real estate investing. It is lead by Scott McGillivray (from the hit TV show "Income Property") and his business partner Michael Sarracini. Michael said something one day that really resonated with me regarding our mindset towards spending or investing money. He said, "It's not about how much something costs, it's about what you are going to get in return." It's called your ROI or Return on Investment. When you invest in yourself, you will always benefit.

Brilliance in Action:

Who could give you guidance to help you achieve your goals?

Find a coach, teacher or mentor that can help be your "Guiding Light". Ask them for help.

Use their time wisely by preparing questions in advance.

Regroup with your coach, teacher or mentor when you have completed their recommendations so that you can discuss your progress and determine your next steps.

Book LIGHTS – Back to Basics

You don't always need to spend large sums of money to invest in coaching. A lot of my learning has been done through the reading of great books. When I read, I pull out the golden nuggets, and determine if and how I can apply a certain principle or tactic in my life. And then I determine how I can share these principles with others.

Being a consistent reader is one of the best things you can do for yourself. Reading for at least one hour a day is one of my "Habits of Brilliance". I must admit I am addicted to books - I love spending time in book stores. Often I come home with 2-3 books at a time. I own all my books (no borrowing from the library) so I can mark them up as I consume the knowledge they provide. I am building an amazing library – something I can pass down to my kids so that they can continue their own journey to brilliance.

I usually have 5 books at any given time that I am working through. Books on productivity, psychology, economics and finance, leadership and personal development. Because I love to read and want to be able to do more of it, one of my development goals is learning to speed read. That way, I can devour more content in less time. The other thing I do is subscribe to book summary services. They take some of the most popular books and summarize them into an 8 page document which takes about 20 minutes to read. If the content is really good in the summary, I often buy the book.

Read what you enjoy. Find subjects that interest you and read about them. When you read, you expand your knowledge and grow yourself – and that makes you more valuable in the world. When you share your learnings with others and help them grow and develop – well that's just brilliant!

Find ways to continue learning. You can take courses, attend conferences and lectures or even listen to audio programs in your car. Make learning one of your "Habits of Brilliance" for your lifetime!

Brilliance in Action:

Define your current habits as they relate to continuous learning - write them down.

If you're not already an avid reader, find at least one book that supports one of the big goals you want to accomplish. Commit to completing that book over the next month.

See my website www.thelightbulbstrategy.com for a list of books that I have found to be brilliant.

Robert Craig

Get Support from Blue LIGHTS

I was with my family just outside of Kapuskasing one weekend, visiting my wife's parents. My son got sick and we took him to the hospital in town. During our long wait at the hospital, the weather was getting bad. Snow was coming down faster than I had seen in a long time. When we finally finished up at the hospital we headed to the edge of town to journey back to my wife's parents when we were brought to an abrupt halt. In front of us was a long line of cars and trucks on the highway. The highway had been closed due to the extreme weather. Now what were we going to do? It was getting dark and we wanted to get back to the house. We parked our car and wandered around a nearby Walmart. Finally, we got word that the highway had been reopened. Blue lights lit up the night sky. Snow plows arrived and helped clear a path so we could find our way to our destination – home.

Blue Lights represent the support you will need to achieve your goals. Just like a snow plow that helps to clear a path, people who support you and help you achieve your goals are Blue Lights. You need to develop "Blue Light Thinking".

"Blue Lights" can help support you directly in achieving your goals. They can also support you in achieving your goals indirectly. If you delegate tasks that are not part of your goals, it frees up your time to work on tasks that will help you achieve your goals.

For example, if you run a small business you may be wearing many different hats to complete all the tasks you require to keep your business running. Hiring a bookkeeper to keep your records straight instead of spending your valuable time doing it is - "Blue Light Thinking".

The Light Bulb Strategy

Hiring a neighborhood kid to cut your grass instead of spending your valuable time doing it is "Blue Light Thinking" – I think you get the picture.

Brilliance in Action:

Exercise: "Blue Light Thinking"

What activities in your life could you delegate to others so that you free up your time for what is most important? List these activities on a piece of paper.

Elements of Brilliance

When you have your goal clearly defined you need to build a strategic plan on how you are going to go about achieving it. So, how do you start? By listing your "Elements of Brilliance."

The task of starting to develop a plan can be overwhelming. I always suggest starting by creating a list of things you need to do and resources you're going to require in order to achieve your vision. This list will become your "Elements of Brilliance" and give you the necessary things to get you started.

It's like building a recipe from scratch. You need a list of ingredients and the instructions to put it all together. Here we are defining what those ingredients (elements) are.

For example, we may need flour and eggs for the recipe, but we may also need a fully equipped kitchen to put all the ingredients together. The key here is to get all the things down on paper and out of your head. List all the things you can think of that you will need – whether you have them already or not.

Part of my vision (and my wife's!) was to have a Florida vacation home for our family. We wanted to have a place where we could spend the winter months during our retirement. Our vision is to have our kids visit us with our grandchildren (not that we have any grandchildren yet – it is part of our future vision though!) and take them to see the great attractions Florida has to offer.

Our goal to purchase a house in Florida was going to be a lot of work, but we knew in the end it would all be worth it. The question was, "Where do we start?" We started to write a list of things we were going to need. An example of some of the priority things we needed to purchase a house in Florida are listed here.

Things we would need included:

- Down payment for the house
- Mortgage with a U.S. bank
- An excellent credit rating (so we could qualify for the mortgage)
- Time to view/review properties and manage all the activities required to purchase a property (filling out forms, applications, etc.)

Also, we would require people to help us through all stages of the real estate deal – these would include both our Guiding Lights and our supportive Blue Lights:

- Bank Mortgage Officer to pre-approve our purchase price and help us with our mortgage application and closing on the deal.
- Real Estate Agent to help us find the right property and help us with a purchase agreement to secure the property
- Real Estate Lawyer to provide us with advice on how to

structure ourselves to properly purchase the property and close on the deal.
- Insurance Broker to ensure we had the proper insurance in place
- Inspector to check the property to make sure we knew what we were going to buy
- Tax accountant to ensure our filing with the various tax authorities was properly done
- Property Manager to take care of the property after the deal closed

As part of our list, we also listed what additional knowledge we would require (questions we would need answers for):

- What kind of mortgage can I get in the U.S.?
- How is the Florida real estate market growing?
- What communities should we be looking in?
- How can I rent out my property when I am not using it?
- What are the steps to purchasing a U.S. property?
- Should we look at short sales or foreclosures?

One of the forms you can use as part of *The Light Bulb Strategy* is the "Elements of Brilliance" list. A sample of this form is also available on my website for you to download at www.TheLightBulbStrategy.com

You use this form by first answering the question, "What do you want to do?" In my example, I have written, "Buy a Florida Vacation home". Then you can brainstorm all the different elements you will need to complete this goal. The first section is to list all the **things** you will need. Then you can list the **people** you will need to help accomplish what you want. Finally, there is a section where you can list the **skills/knowledge** you will need so you can keep moving forward.

Robert Craig

Elements of Brilliance

What do you want to do? Buy a Florida Vacation home

What things will you need to do this?

Down payment for house	Mortgage with U.S. bank	Excellent Credit Rating	Time to review/view Properties

Who do you need to help you do this?

Bank Mortgage Officer	Real Estate Agent	Lawyer	Property Manager
Tax Accountant	Insurance Broker	House Inspector	

What skills/knowledge do you need to do this?

U.S. mortgages – types, rates?	Florida real estate market conditions? Growing?	Type of structure to purchase U.S. property?	Consider Foreclosures?
What area of Florida to buy in?	Impact of exchange rates?		

The Light Bulb Strategy

Brilliance in Action:

Exercise: "Elements of Brilliance"

What do you want to do? *Put your goal at the top of the page.*

List out all the things you will need, people who can help you and what knowledge/skills you will require.

An alternative approach to get your thoughts onto paper is to use an idea or mind map. Mind mapping is a great tool that allows you to see visually all the elements involved in a subject and how they link and associate together.

To create a mind map, write your vision in the center of a piece of paper and start putting ideas that stem out from the center of all the things you can think of that you would need to do to achieve your goal. I also suggest that you use mind mapping software. That way you can easily move ideas around your mind map as you think through all the elements of your vision. I often use my iPad to mind map things. I like that I can add items and easily move them around the screen with my finger so they can link up with other items on the map.

By having all the elements required to achieve your goal in front of you, you will get a better picture of the gap that exists between where you are today and where you want to be. It also gives you a starting place to sequence activities so that you can focus on certain elements as priorities.

If your goal is complex, you may find it beneficial to break your goal requirements into separate lists or mind maps.

Elements of Brilliance
Idea Map

- What do you want to do?
  - What things will you need?
  - Who do you need to help you?
  - What skills or knowledge do you need?

The Light Bulb Strategy

SWOT your Elements of Brilliance

Once you have created your "Elements of Brilliance" list or map, you need to scan your list to determine the status of each element. Do you have this element in hand or is there work to be done to get it?

One common method to do this kind of determination is through a SWOT analysis. SWOT is an acronym for **S**trengths, **W**eaknesses, **O**pportunities and **T**hreats. This is another great tool to help you determine where to focus your efforts and set goals. This is where you really start to think strategically on the best approach going forward with the limited resources you have (Time, Money, Energy).

Your Strengths section would list things you already have that will help you move towards achieving your vision. These are items such as resources, special skills you may have that distinguish you from other people or even competitors. These are things that can give you an advantage.

Your Weaknesses are areas where you are vulnerable. These items could be potential roadblocks that could get in your way of achieving your vision. There could be a certain skill you lack or there could be other behavioral factors (refer back to Chapter 1 where we discussed some of these – i.e. The 60 Watt Light bulb – your limiting beliefs).

Your Opportunities are possible situations where you could benefit. For example, if you own a bakery, one of your main ingredients would be flour. If there was a plentiful wheat harvest, there may be an opportunity to buy in bulk to save money.

Your Threats are possible situations which could jeopardize your efforts to achieve your vision. For example, the wheat harvest may have been bad which may result in higher prices for flour – this could impede your bakery business. These factors are outside of your control. The key thing here is to identify as many threats as possible – to gain awareness.

A SWOT analysis is typically done in a table format with your Strengths and Weaknesses first. These fall under the first row as Internal Factors. Internal meaning we have some control of their outcome. The second row is for Opportunities and Threats. These are External Factors – because we don't have control over them.

Our Strengths & Opportunities fall under the positive column – These are items that are good and give us positive energy. Our Weaknesses and Threats fall under the negative column – These are items that are not good and provide negative energy.

Looking at your SWOT, you could see an identified strength and draw a line to an opportunity that you could go after. You could also identify a strength that could be used to mitigate one of your weaknesses.

The SWOT analysis provides us with greater clarity on positive items that we could leverage and negative items that we could choose to mitigate. In either case, the SWOT will allow us to choose what to focus on and set goals to move towards our vision.

As I mentioned before, we were looking to buy a vacation property in Florida. After listing all of the Elements of Brilliance, you can start adding these Elements to your SWOT analysis. You will also add other items to your SWOT that can affect your vision. I have included an example of my SWOT for buying our vacation property in the attached figure.

SWOT - Your "Elements of Brilliance"

What do you want to do? __Buy a Florida Vacation home__

	Positive	*Negative*
Internal	**Strengths** - Have a strong desire to own a property in Florida - Have a down payment for house - Have an excellent credit rating to help get financing	**Weaknesses** - No experience buying U.S. properties - Don't have a real estate agent in Florida - Need to get mortgage in the U.S. - Have never filed with the IRS before
External	**Opportunities** - Exchange rate near par - House prices in Florida dropped dramatically since 2008 recession - U.S. economy now seems to be growing	**Threats** - Interest rates could go up - Property could be damaged by extreme weather (hurricanes, flooding) - May have problems getting vacation renters

The Light Bulb Strategy

Using the SWOT analysis for buying a Florida vacation home helped us clarify that it was the right time to purchase. We had our down payment, interest rates were low, the exchange rate was close to par and there were signs that the U.S. economy was recovering.

The SWOT also showed us where we would need to get further educated and do our proper due diligence. We were going to have to learn how to buy property in the U.S.; how to organize ourselves to make the purchase. We would also need to build our team that would help us through the entire process. It further showed that we would need to put plans in place to help mitigate the threats we identified. For example, our concern of property damage would be mitigated by putting the proper insurance policy in place.

Now it's time to build your own SWOT for what you want to do to realize your vision.

<u>Brilliance in Action:</u>

Exercise – SWOT your "Elements of Brilliance"

Pull out a SWOT template – one is provided at www.TheLightBulbStrategy.com

Under the Strengths space, list all the things you have going for you in achieving your vision.

Under the Weakness space, list all the things you don't have that could hold you back from achieving your vision.

Under the Opportunities space, list things that are happening around you in your environment that could help you achieve your vision.

Under the Threats space, list things that are happening around you in your environment that could hinder your ability to achieve your vision.

Next, we will use elements from our SWOT to help us set some short term goals and sequence priorities – HOW we are going to do WHAT we want to do!

Brilliant Goals

At the end of the second chapter I talked about how to write SMART goals (which is a very well-known approach to goal setting). After you have completed your SWOT analysis exercise (SWOT your Elements of Brilliance), you will want to define some goals that will move you towards achieving your vision.

Hopefully your SWOT template provides you with a clearer picture of what you need to do. Say, for example your SWOT identified to you that one of your weaknesses was that you lacked a certain skill. If you determined that in order to achieve your vision, you will need this skill, then you may decide as part of your strategy to take a course, read a book or talk to an expert on the subject.

A goal statement may look something like this:
"By September 1, I will start a bookkeeping course at my local college and achieve a grade of at least 90%."

This goal is Specific – you want to start a bookkeeping course at a local college. It is Measurable – you want a grade of at least 90%. Notice it does not say you want to achieve a grade of 90% - if you achieve 92% then you did not achieve your goal of getting 90%. By writing that you want to get at least 90% you correctly identify what you want.

Is the target of getting at least 90% Attainable? Is your goal Relevant? Will bookkeeping help you to achieve your Vision? Perhaps you could hire someone to do your bookkeeping instead of learning it yourself. Or perhaps you want to take bookkeeping so you understand how basic finances of a business work. Finally, is the goal Time Bound? This goal says that by September 1 you will have started the course – so, yes, it is time bound.

For our Florida vacation home, one of our goals was to better educate ourselves in purchasing U.S. real estate. The fact that we had no experience purchasing U.S. real estate was a weakness noted in our SWOT. So we put together a goal to better educate ourselves on the process.

Our Brilliant Goal of becoming better educated on U.S. real estate is:

"By July 31, we will have conducted our due diligence process of understanding how to purchase U.S. real estate. We will have read and reviewed at least three books, attended bank seminars and workshops and will have consulted experts on the subject including bankers, lawyers and real estate agents."

As you continue through your SWOT analysis, you will identify other goals to work on – be sure to write them down.

Once your goals are defined, you need to put a plan in place to get working on them. To do that, you must put first things first – to sequence them. As you can't do all your goals at once, determine which goals are most important and put them at the top of the list to work on.

The Light Bulb Strategy

LIGHT Sequence

Have you ever been to a fireworks show? I'm sure you have. They can be spectacular. A few years ago, I took my family to Walt Disney World in Florida. We were at Epcot one night for the fireworks show. When the sun went down the anticipation grew as everyone found their spot to get the greatest view of the show that was about to start in the sky.

Finally, the sky lit up with an amazing array of colors. Music was part of the show and perfectly timed to the explosion of the fireworks – Amazing!

Think about the work that needs to be done to get a show like this to happen. It needs to be planned to the utmost detail and then executed flawlessly in order to achieve their goal of wowing their audience. They need to have in place a sequence of events – which fireworks go off when? What order do they go? Which fireworks are fired at the same time as other fireworks?

In order to achieve our goals, we need to do the same thing and sequence our activities (tasks) that will drive us towards achieving the goal.

Some activities can be done in parallel – working on multiple things at the same time. Other activities may be dependent on another activity being completed first. Plan the activities that need to be done by putting them in priority order.

You need the discipline to get the first thing done and then move on to the next thing and get it done. As you keep working on getting activities done you see progress which will motivate you to keep going and drive towards achieving your goal.

As Mark Twain said, "The secret of getting ahead is getting started. The secret to getting started is breaking your complex overwhelming tasks into small manageable tasks and the starting on the first one."

When we bought our vacation rental house in Florida, we had to break down the overall goal of Florida home ownership into smaller activities. We had a lot of homework to do. Financially, we needed to understand what we could afford before we started looking at houses. What amount of mortgage would the bank approve us for? Once we knew the mortgage amount along with our down payment requirements we could start looking at potential houses to buy. But before we could start looking at houses we had to find a real estate agent!

Like I mentioned earlier in the chapter, the best way I have learned to start sequencing activities is to use mind mapping.

Again, a mind map starts by putting your main theme in the center of the page. Then you create idea branches that come out from the center main theme. For our Florida home purchase, I created a center circle and called it "Florida Rental Vacation Home". Then, I put sub-circle branches all around the center circle and labelled them, "Find a house", "Buy the house", "Close on the house", "Set up the house", "Rent out the house", "Maintain the house". Then from these sub-circle branches, I added additional sub-branches. For example, under the branch "Buy the house" we need to ensure we had proper "financing", – which involved having the proper "down payment" as well as getting a "mortgage" "pre-approval" and also understanding the various "types" of mortgages.

The mind map really helped us define all the things we needed to consider and put plans in place to make it happen. More importantly, the map allowed us to see what activities needed to

The Light Bulb Strategy

be done before other dependent activities could be completed. It allowed us to put in order and prioritize our next critical step – taking action.

But before we get into the action/execution step, let's first talk about protecting our light bulb so that we can sustain our brilliance on the way to achieving our goals.

5

The Light Bulb Strategy Blueprint

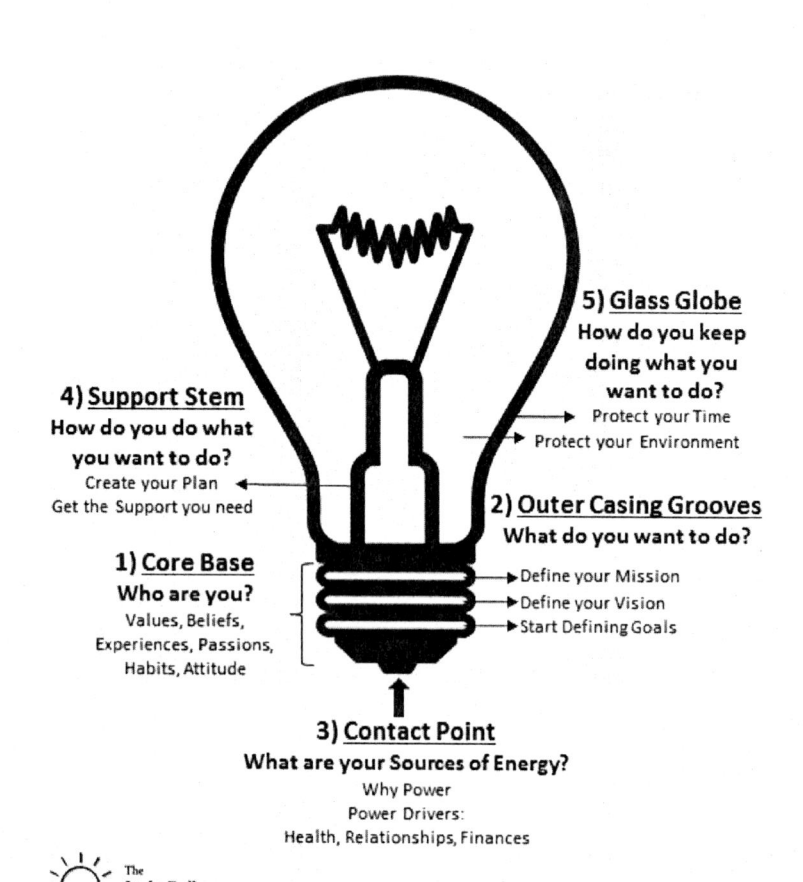

5) Glass Globe
How do you keep doing what you want to do?
→ Protect your Time
→ Protect your Environment

4) Support Stem
How do you do what you want to do?
Create your Plan
Get the Support you need

2) Outer Casing Grooves
What do you want to do?
→ Define your Mission
→ Define your Vision
→ Start Defining Goals

1) Core Base
Who are you?
Values, Beliefs, Experiences, Passions, Habits, Attitude

3) Contact Point
What are your Sources of Energy?
Why Power
Power Drivers:
Health, Relationships, Finances

The Light Bulb Strategy

"A man who dares to waste one hour of time has not discovered the value of life."
                                                            Charles Darwin

Step 5

PROTECT YOUR LIGHT BULB

"Safeguard and Sustain your Brilliance."

On "The Light Bulb Strategy Blueprint", the next part of the light bulb is the glass globe that completes the housing of the light bulb. The glass globe itself represents time – WHEN you will get things done. Time is fixed, once it is used up, it is gone forever; - we cannot get it back.

The fifth step of "The Light Bulb Strategy" is to protect your light bulb so that you can safeguard and sustain WHAT you want to do.

At the Speed of LIGHT - Time

Comedian Steven Wright once said, "If you are in a spaceship that is traveling at the speed of light, and you turn on the headlights, does anything happen?"

I grew up loving science fiction - stories with time machines that could bring you to the past or the future. Movies where space ships travel at incredible speeds from one galaxy to another using LIGHT speed. The amount of time we could save if we had that kind of technology today.

As I have gotten older, I have realized the importance of managing time. It is a limited resource that we need to protect well. They say if you lose money you can always make it back, but when you lose time, you can never get it back.

It is incredible the amount of time people waste. They waste time doing unimportant things or things they think are important, but in reality are not. In our fast paced world, even with the help of great technology, it is easy to get thrown around from one thing to the other – competing priorities, work commitments, family commitments, trying to check-off that never ending to-do list. All of this can leave us quite frustrated and overwhelmed.

How much of your precious time do you spend in front of monitors? TV monitors, computer monitors and smart phones? A lot of people question why they are not getting ahead in life. One reason is that they are spending a lot of their valuable time in front of their TV. There's nothing wrong with watching TV; we just need to monitor the amount of time we do it.

Sitting in front of our computer monitors is another way we can lose valuable time if we don't monitor the amount of time we spend. When we spend countless hours mindlessly surfing the net for recreation or playing video games it has a dramatic effect on our productivity. We have become so distracted, our time is wasted, our dimmer switch drops low – our brilliance fades.

I saw a t-shirt the other day and it made me chuckle and shake my head. It said "The internet is broken so I'm outside today." We have become addicted to our smart phones. Technology today has transformed the way we communicate – which is good and bad. It's good because we can stay better connected to the ones we love through calling, emailing, texting, Skyping and face timing. It's bad because now anybody can have instant access to you and your precious time.

The Light Bulb Strategy

Because we live in a world where people have easier access to us, we need to be even more diligent in how we manage and protect our time. A huge lesson we must learn is how to say "No." That's right – repeat after me and say "No." No to that unimportant meeting, no to that unimportant invite.

The problem here is that we tend to be people pleasers; – we don't like to disappoint others so we say yes to unimportant events and activities so as not to impact negatively on relationships. In Greg McKeown's book, *Essentialism, The Disciplined Pursuit of Less*, he had this to say about saying no. "The potential upside, however, [of saying no] is less obvious: when the initial annoyance or disappointment or anger wears off, the respect kicks in. When we push back effectively, it shows people that our time is highly valuable. It distinguishes the professional from the amateur."

Sun LIGHT, Moon LIGHT... Earth LIGHT

We all have 24 hours in a day – every one of us. How we use those hours is so critical. To be brilliant, we need to get a hold of our schedule and be proactive in managing our time. Now, I am not saying you need to manage every hour of your life, but you should schedule your time for what is most important.

So what is most important? Focusing your light on the most important activities to achieve your goals and vision. Once you have determined the activities you will focus on, you need to get them scheduled into your calendar.

The sun, moon and the earth are the foundation of how our calendar works. The month is related to the motion of the moon, our days are related to the earth's rotation with the sun and our years are related to the earth revolving around the sun.

These celestial relationships are part of the laws of nature in which we belong. These natural relationships give us a great system to plan and live our life to the fullest. We can establish annual goals and then break them down into monthly and daily goals.

To be successful you need to think big, but you also need to think small. Working small is the big idea here. A year is big, but in relation to a year, a day is small. You need to look at your goals - daily. You need to work on your goals - daily. You need to plan your calendar so that you schedule things that need to get done, - get done - daily. Sure you have regular daily tasks and errands to get done, but you need to focus on making the time to work on your goals daily. Do something, anything that will move you forward towards your goals.

If your goal is to get in better shape, a daily goal may be to buy a book about fitness and nutrition or joining a gym, hiring a fitness trainer, going for a walk. The important thing is to write it down in your calendar and then do it!

Your family is important; - ensure you are scheduling quality time with them. Don't let your time slip away. Plan vacations and fun family activities. Put these in your calendar, block off the time and protect these very important activities.

The Light Bulb Strategy

<u>Brilliance in Action:</u>

Exercise – "Protect your Time"

What could you do with an extra hour a day?

What unproductive activities could you say "no" to so that you could gain an extra hour a day?

Find a calendar system that works for you – a date book, on your tablet or smart phone and use it consistently.

Block off time for your most important things – book your vacation time, time with your family, activities that support your most important goals.

LIGHT up your World - Environment

The interior of the glass bubble represents WHERE you will get things done, or more specifically your environment. The inert gas in the bulb allows it to glow, like oxygen!

The environment in which you operate as an individual is so critical to your success. When your environment is rich, it allows your light bulb to shine brilliantly! The brilliant light shines from the light bulb and extends beyond the glass bulb out into the world. The brighter the bulb shines, the greater impact you are having on achieving your goals, your vision and your mission.

What kind of environment do you physically live in? Is your home, work place organized or cluttered? When you work and live in a cluttered environment it depletes your energy and can have a huge impact on your overall mood.

My wife and I have identified that de-cluttering the house is one of our top goals. We recognize that our moods are directly related to the state our home is in. And with three teenagers coming and going all the time, we need to be on top of the de-cluttering mission.

We are constantly looking through our closets and storage bins for clothing we no longer need or use. We sort through the piles and determine what gets thrown out or donated.

We rummaged through our storage room and purged what we no longer needed. We had garage sales to move our unwanted home inventory. Whatever didn't sell was donated – no way was it coming back in to the house!

When you clear the physical clutter in your life, it gives you such a sense of relief. I suggest you have a goal to clear physical clutter in your life. Choose something small to start with – a cluttered drawer, then move your way up over time to that closet, that storage room, and don't forget that garage.

Brilliance in Action:

Exercise – "Protect your Physical Environment"

Consider establishing a goal to de-clutter your physical environment. Start with something small to get you started. Establish a goal using the SMART criteria.

LIGHT up your Mind

To shine brilliantly to the outer world, we must also protect what we allow into our glass bubble. Negative influences can hinder and even cripple our ability to shine.

The Light Bulb Strategy

Protect what you allow into your mind. There is so much negativity in the world. Don't let this negativity in and dim your light. Find ways to protect what you let in. For example, if you spend a lot of time listening to the news on the radio while you drive or watching news reports on TV, you are exposed to a lot of sensational news that has a negative impact on your mind. Stories of accidents, political corruption, murders do nothing but feed your reptilian brain leaving you both consciously and subconsciously stirring.

So what do you do to protect your light bulb from all this negativity? Limit your exposure to news on the radio, on your TV and in your newspaper. Spend more time reading inspirational books and magazines. Listen to educational audio programs during your commute. Feed your brain the good stuff – good content, brilliant content!

The other way to protect your mind is by de-cluttering your mental environment. It could be a relationship that needs mending, a project that needs finishing, or any other incomplete items in your life. Work to include fixing these incomplete items by adding them to your goals.

Brilliance in Action:

Exercise – "Protect your Mental Environment"

Determine something in your life that you need to complete. That is something you need to fix, finish or possibly mend. Establish a goal using the SMART criteria.

Head LIGHTS and Brake LIGHTS

Be aware of the people you associate with. As Jim Rohn said, "You are the average of the five people you spend the most time with." Do the people you hang around with help move you forward like head lights on a car help move you forward on a dark road? Or do these people slow you down or make you stop like brake lights on a car?

Do the people you associate with discourage you from achieving your dreams? There is a great saying, "The people who say 'you can't' or 'you won't' are the same people who are afraid 'you will'". If you hang around people who are negative, cynical, constantly gossiping about other people, they will have a negative impact on you (they turn down the energy on your dimmer switch).

Hang around people who are working to develop and grow themselves. People who are positive and motivate you. People who have strong values like yours. People who have their own goals, vision and mission. People who are on their own path to success. Work to surround yourself and build relationships with brilliant people who have great ideas. As Eleanor Roosevelt once said, "Great minds discuss ideas; average minds discuss events; small minds discuss people."

Brilliance in Action:

Exercise – "Head Lights and Brake Lights"

Make a list the people you associate with. Then note if they are head lights or brake lights – that is do they move you forward or hold you back?

The Light Bulb Strategy

If your list is full of people who are "Brake Lights", what could you do to limit or eliminate those associations?

List 5 ways to find and develop relationships with "Head Lights".

Shinier LIGHTS

Beyond finding people who motivate and encourage you and propel you forward you also need to find "Shinier Lights" - that is people who are ahead of you and are successful in an area that is important to you (their lights are more brilliant and shinier than yours!). When you hang around "Shinier Lights", the brilliance they share will help your light bulb to shine brilliantly as well. "Surround yourself with who you want to be."

As you build relationships with these people, you may decide you want them to become your mentor,- which we talked about earlier in the book (Your Guiding Lights).

<u>*Brilliance in Action:*</u>

Exercise – "Find Shinier Lights"

Where could you find people who have "Shinier Lights" than you?

Set a goal to find and connect with "Shiner Lights" in an area of your life that you are focusing on – health, relationships, spirituality, personal development, finances or business.

There are many places you might consider to find shinier lights – people at your office, taking a course, attending a conference, joining various associations or organizations, or doing some volunteering in your community.

What if LIGHTning Strikes?

Sometimes storms can hit quickly and with those storms come lightning. The thing about lightning is that it can hit at any time, and anywhere. What can you do to protect yourself if lightning strikes? Have a thought-out plan ready to go.

Part of having a good plan is to plan what to do if things don't go your way. It's called contingency planning and it's critical to think through.

When you put a contingency plan in place it allows you to feel more in control of situations should they occur.

I had the pleasure of seeing Canadian astronaut Chris Hadfield speak at conference about his adventure of journeying to the International Space Station, his work while he was there and his terrifying return trip home.

The Light Bulb Strategy

As an astronaut, Hadfield had to train for all kinds of unlikely events – most of which were life and death situations. In his book, *An Astronaut's Guide to Life on Earth*, he says, "Anticipating problems and figuring out how to solve them is actually the opposite of worrying: it's productive. Likewise, coming up with a plan of action isn't a waste of time if it gives you peace of mind. While it's true that you may wind up being ready for something that never happens, if the stakes are at all high, it's worth it."

Any good project manager will think through "what if" scenarios in what's called a "Risk Register". They would need to determine a course of action they would follow if one of those unfortunate scenarios occurred.

We've all heard the saying, "Hope for the best, plan for the worst." We need to do the same thinking for our personal lives. What would you do if you lost a loved one, lost a job, became sick? Do you have the resources you will need to help you through difficult times?

Pilot LIGHT – try it out first

Sometimes it may be prudent to experiment and try new things to see how they work out. This would be done before you engage fully and start committing your limited resources.

As a Project Manager, I learned it is imperative that you pilot something (a product or service) before you roll it out to the marketplace. That is you need to test it to make sure it works to avoid major rework and recalls at a major expense.

When the company I work for was getting ready to launch our proprietary credit card program, we did a pilot study first. We had a couple of plastic credit cards made and went out to test if they worked. To our dismay, they didn't. We had trouble having the card reader read the imprint on the card. The issue was that the position of the number embossed on the card was incorrect – it was too high on the card. It was my fault as I gave direction to move the height of the embossed imprint to make it match better with the background artwork on the plastic credit card. I learned that the position of the embossing on the card is an industry standard and cannot be changed. So we changed the location of the number embossed on the card and tested it again. It worked perfectly.

But what if this had not been tested? What if we sent out thousands of cards to customers and they didn't work?

Before you go "all-in" on a new endeavor, project or career, try to pilot it somehow to see if it works the way you envisioned.

So, now we know a few things on how to protect ourselves – our time, our environment and our mind. With our goals in hand, now is the time to take our plan and Switch It On!

6

The Light Bulb Strategy Blueprint

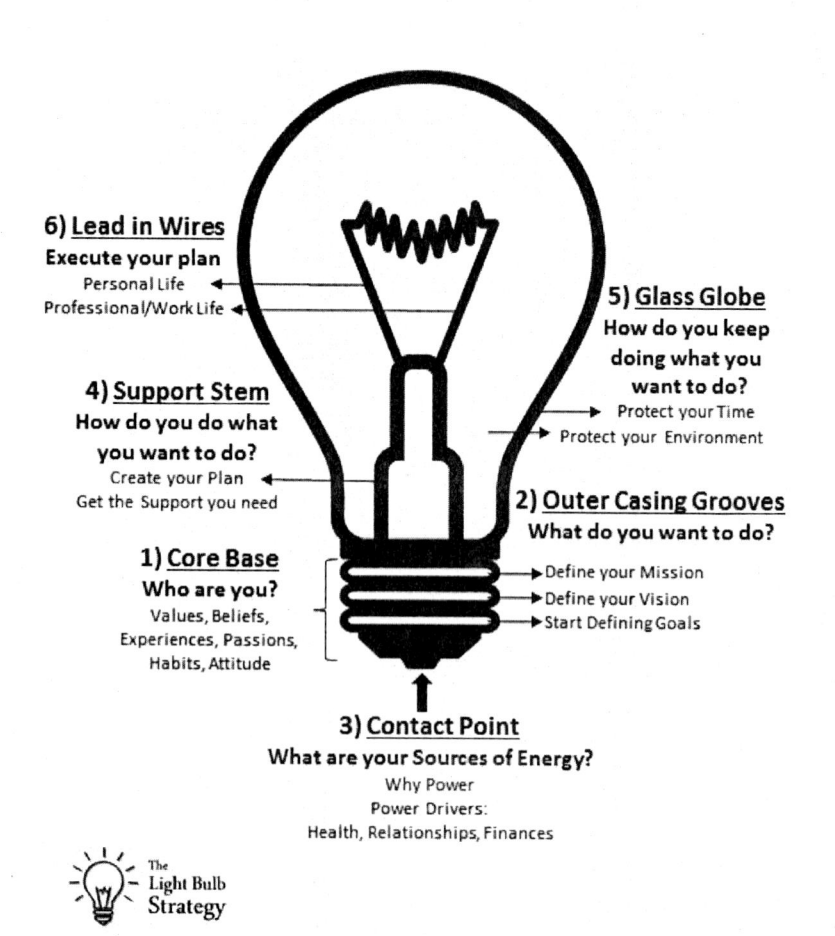

6) Lead in Wires
Execute your plan
 Personal Life
 Professional/Work Life

5) Glass Globe
How do you keep doing what you want to do?
 Protect your Time
 Protect your Environment

4) Support Stem
How do you do what you want to do?
 Create your Plan
 Get the Support you need

2) Outer Casing Grooves
What do you want to do?
 Define your Mission
 Define your Vision
 Start Defining Goals

1) Core Base
Who are you?
 Values, Beliefs,
 Experiences, Passions,
 Habits, Attitude

3) Contact Point
What are your Sources of Energy?
 Why Power
 Power Drivers:
 Health, Relationships, Finances

The Light Bulb Strategy

"A journey of a thousand miles must begin with a single step."
                                                  Chinese proverb

Step 6

SWITCH-ON YOUR LIGHT BULB
"It's time to Show your Brilliance!"

My wife is a master at getting things done. Once she sets her mind to get something done, she jumps into action. Let me give you an example:

One of her goals has always been to get a dog for our family. Her roadblock - was me! "I'm allergic to dogs!" As a child I suffered anytime we went to visit family and friends who had pets - cats, dogs - if it had fur, it made my eyes water and greatly hindered my ability to breathe normally.

The conversation came up during morning coffee on a Saturday; "I think we should get a puppy - what do you think?"
"I'm allergic to dogs – I don't think it's a good idea" I countered.
"I know you're allergic - that's why we are going to get a hypo-allergenic dog so you won't have a problem. Have you ever been around a hypo-allergenic dog?"
"Ahhh...no, what kind of dog did you have in mind?" I asked.
"A Yorkshire Terrier." she quickly answered.
"Okay, – I'm happy to start doing some homework on Yorkshire Terriers then," I said.
By 4:00 that afternoon, I was sitting in a stranger's house looking to buy their newly acquired Yorkshire Terrier that they decided they no longer wanted to keep. My wife and three boys watched me with hopeful eyes as I raised the dog to my nose

for the allergic "sniff test". I was fine - no issues. By 7:00 that evening I had a new Yorkshire Terrier living in my house. My wife named him Pinot - yes that's right, named after the wine Pinot Grigio, my wife's favorite white wine. Pinot is now a very important part of our family - he's a great dog. Even greater because I can still breathe around him!

LIGHTS, Camera, Action!

The sub-title of this book says to take the Light Bulb Strategy and "Switch it On". The "Switch it On" part is all about taking action - you need to do something. In order for you to light up a light bulb, you need to switch it on. You need to execute to get Illumination – to show your brilliance!

The sixth step of "The Light Bulb Strategy" is to Switch On your light bulb and take action by doing what you want to do.

If you have a great plan but you don't execute on it, it is worthless. If you execute, but you don't have a plan, your time could be wasted. The right strategic plan multiplied by focused persistent execution leads to effective results!

Let's get back to "The Light Bulb Strategy Blueprint". There are two wires that come up from the base in a light bulb; - these wires connect to the filament to make it glow. For the light bulb metaphor, the left wire represents your personal life and the right wire represents your professional/work life. When you get your personal life in balance with your professional/work life, the filament glows brilliantly. If the balance is compromised, the filament may not shine very brilliantly.

The Light Bulb Strategy

For example, if you are working all the time and neglect your family, missing that dance recital or those little league baseball games, after a while it will catch up, especially if that personal time is not made up.

In the previous chapter, we reviewed the importance of planning and prioritizing our time. Now we are at the point where it's time to execute. Execution of the plan starts with what you are going to do now – today. How are you going to ensure you get done the most important things? What is in the spotlight today?

The SpotLIGHT

During live stage productions there are many lights that shine on the stage so we can see the performers and the set. The spotlight focuses down onto the main performer and follows them around the stage as they move. The spotlight highlights for us what we should be focusing our attention on. To be productive, we need to do the same thing and adopt "Spotlight Thinking". That is, you need to determine your priority, focus on it and keep with it! Ask yourself, "What's in the spotlight today?"

To do this, write a list of the most important things that need to get done at the beginning of your day. Then identify which order they should be done and then get working on them. You need to list both personal and work/professional related items.

When the first performer has completed their act, the next performer comes out and the spotlight changes over to the new performer. Just like performers, when you have completed work on your first priority move onto the next priority and focus on it. This focus on priorities is the key to getting results!

You often hear people talk about being great multitaskers. That is, they can work on multiple things at once. This may seem like a great skill to have, but in reality it just slows you down. The reason is every time you switch from one task to another, your brain needs time to adjust and refocus which uses up energy. As David Rock says in his book, *Your Brain at Work*, "While you can hold several chunks of information in mind at once, you can't perform more than one conscious process at a time with these chunks without impacting performance." Rock recommends that you "catch yourself trying to do two things at once and slow down instead." And if you have to multi-task, "combine active thinking tasks only with automatic embedded routines." Those automatic embedded routines are things you do with little conscious effort – they are the routines that are stored in the basal ganglia part of your brain.

A String of LIGHTS

Sometimes it's hard just getting started. We delay, defer and procrastinate. This is where "String of Light" thinking can help. A String of Lights has many small lights, but when you put a bunch of these small lights together they can produce a lot of light.

The Light Bulb Strategy

Starting small gets you going. When you get going and get something done that is working towards your goals, you feel good. Your brains neurotransmitter - dopamine is activated, which helps control the brain's reward and pleasure centers. By accomplishing a goal, - even a small one, dopamine rewards you. Then momentum kicks in and gives you the motivation you need to continue on to the next item.

In his book, *The One Thing,* Gary Keller says, "The prescription for extraordinary results is knowing what matters to you and taking daily doses of action in alignment with it."

So start small, get going and work daily on your goals. The accumulation of all your small goal achievements along your "String of Lights" will help lead you to brilliance.

The FlashLIGHT

As you work on your goals, you won't be able to predict everything you will need to do, but that's part of the fun! As you make the journey to achieve your goals, unexpected things are going to happen as you progress along - life happens!

It's like walking along a path at night; - as you walk along, the flashlight only reveals so much of the path ahead. As you walk you may encounter obstacles you weren't expecting – a tree that has fallen in your path; a river that you must determine how to cross. The same thing happens when you are working towards achieving your goals. As you progress, things are going to happen that will block your path or knock you off course. Don't let these things discourage you; - accept them. Determine the best way to go around, over or through these obstacles. Make the necessary course corrections and move on. Remember, these obstacles and curve balls that life throws at you are all tests to see how truly committed you are to achieving your goal. There is a Japanese proverb, "Fall down seven times, stand up eight."

Again, they key thing is to start – to turn on your flashlight, move forward and start to unveil the path towards your success and brilliance.

Construction LIGHTS

Where I live we have four seasons - winter, fall, spring and Highway Construction! Driving along the highway late at night you encounter traffic! Traffic comes to a standstill as four lanes get reduced down to one. Large construction equipment chews up the ground to make way for road improvements - what a mess! But that mess is necessary! Gradually over time the mess will be gone and a new road will be paved.

When you are in the process of achieving your goals it will be messy, chaotic and stressful. Accept that as part of the journey as well.

When my wife and I decided to get our first income rental property, we did a lot of homework (planning) but then after much review and due diligence it was time to execute on our plan and make it happen – to take action – to "Switch On" the plan.

The first investment property my wife and I bought was back in 2011. The process of buying the property happened faster than I expected. We met our real estate agent on Monday to discuss properties that were for sale that met our criteria. We saw the house we selected on Tuesday, and by Wednesday we had the offer signed and countersigned. Coincidentally, the deal was signed on our wedding anniversary date - quite the gift we had just bought for each other!

We knew the house was going to need a lot of work as it had not been updated for about 30 years. We started planning the renovations that were going to be required as we had a bit of time before we took possession of the property.

We put together a budget on how much the renovations were going to cost. We wanted to do all the renovations for under $25k. We detailed the work that needed to be done on a spreadsheet and determined the order things needed to be done and set priorities. We lined up the people we would need to help us complete the renovations (our blue lights). We were also planning to do much of the work ourselves – build some sweat equity!

The first thing I wanted to do when we got possession of the new house was to remove an old stove in the kitchen that was ancient – it had been there forever. I pulled it out to unplug it and noticed a thick wire ran under the counter cabinets – are you kidding me? The stove was hardwired to the electrical panel. After the stove was finally removed, we started to work on the cabinets. We thought we were just going to paint them but then discovered they were falling apart. So we ended up replacing the kitchen cabinets which was not in our budget. It was a good thing we set aside extra funds in our budget for the unexpected.

Everything was going fine with the renovations, even though they were taking longer than expected. It was when we started working on the bathroom that I had my out of body experience. Let me explain…

I removed the old tub surround walls and started removing the rotten drywall behind. I was wearing my protective goggles (safety first!) and my ventilation mask. You want to talk about sweat; I was drenched. The tub was full of drywall debris, my mask was steaming up making it hard to see – dust particles floating all through the air. Then it happened, the out of body experience. I looked around (of course I could not see much because my mask steamed up and dust particles filled the air) and wondered, "What have we done?" I shook my head in disbelief that we had spent all this money to take on this project. I started to laugh to myself which reminded me of that movie scene in "The Money Pit". There is a scene where the two main characters played by Tom Hanks and Shelley Long go to fill their bathtub and as they fill it, the floor opens up and the bathtub falls through and shatters on the floor below. Tom Hank's character starts to giggle, then laughs hysterically – well that was me. I couldn't control my emotions.

When we were all finished our renovations, the home looked great. The sense of accomplishment was incredible. We had the house re-appraised and it was now worth $60k more that we paid for it. Not bad! That's forced appreciation!

Construction Lights are all about understanding that starting a change is difficult no matter what it is that you are working on – a renovation, a project or making change to improve yourself. When you are in the middle of the transformation it can be very difficult, even to the point of being chaotic. But that is part of the process; the price to pay. You need to stay focused and be persistent. You need to have grit! When you get through the chaos and the frustration, you can look back at what you have done and enjoy your success. And that is what we will do next – Reflect on your Brilliance!

7

The Light Bulb Strategy Blueprint

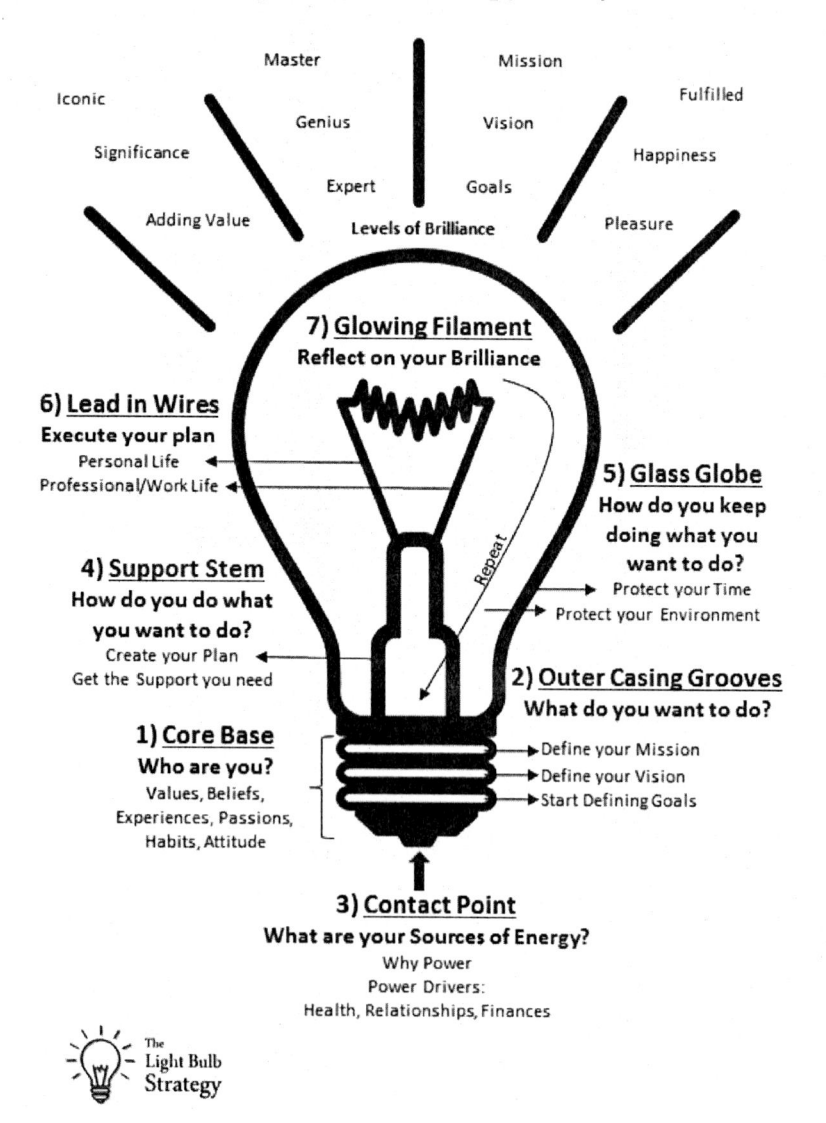

Levels of Brilliance:
- Iconic
- Master
- Significance
- Genius
- Mission
- Vision
- Expert
- Goals
- Fulfilled
- Adding Value
- Happiness
- Pleasure

7) Glowing Filament
Reflect on your Brilliance

6) Lead in Wires
Execute your plan
- Personal Life
- Professional/Work Life

5) Glass Globe
How do you keep doing what you want to do?
- Protect your Time
- Protect your Environment

4) Support Stem
How do you do what you want to do?
- Create your Plan
- Get the Support you need

2) Outer Casing Grooves
What do you want to do?
- Define your Mission
- Define your Vision
- Start Defining Goals

1) Core Base
Who are you?
Values, Beliefs, Experiences, Passions, Habits, Attitude

3) Contact Point
What are your Sources of Energy?
Why Power
Power Drivers:
Health, Relationships, Finances

The Light Bulb Strategy

"If you light a lamp for someone else it will also brighten your path."
Unknown

Step 7

REFLECT ON THE BRILLIANCE FROM YOUR LIGHT BULB

"Blinded by that Brilliant Light Bulb!"

A key part of your success comes from reflecting on how things are going. Taking time to reflect by taking yourself out of your hectic schedule and determining what's working and what's not working. If you can't measure something, you can't manage it properly. If you can't manage it properly, you can't determine how to improve it.

The seventh step of "The Light Bulb Strategy" is to reflect on the brilliance from your light bulb so that you can see and understand your progress toward achieving your WHAT.

Reflected LIGHT

Reflecting on your brilliance is so important. You need to ensure you are on the correct path towards accomplishing your goals, vision and mission. The experience and knowledge you gain along your journey is so valuable. As author and speaker John C. Maxwell says in his book, *The 15 Invaluable Laws of Growth*, "If we don't take the time to pause and reflect, we can miss the significance of such events. Reflection allows those experiences to move from being life markers to life makers."

If you are not getting the results you are looking for, you need to spend some time reflecting on why. You may need to change some of your behaviors to improve your results.

One way to find out what behaviors need improving is by getting feedback from other people. You need to ask them to tell you ways you can improve. Ask them lots of questions like the Traffic Light questions I talked about earlier in the book. "What should I start doing or do more of?" and "What should I stop doing or do less of?"

Many people don't like to get feedback because they are afraid of what they may hear. It takes you right out of your comfort zone, but you must work past your ego and seek feedback so you can grow. When you get this feedback (good or bad), thank the person that provided it – then reflect on it. Think about it. Then determine what action you can take to improve as a result of this feedback.

Track LIGHTS

How often should you reflect on your progress? It all depends on the goals you have set for yourself. If you have an immediate goal of eating better, you would be tracking that daily and measuring your progress by noting what food you are putting in your mouth. If you have longer term goals you may want to check-in and reflect on your progress monthly. If you have big goals and have broken them down into smaller goals, you may want to track them separately.

Tracking your progress is critical to your success. It allows you to see if you are on the right path. And when you are on the right path and you are seeing results, you gain momentum which keeps you going. If you are not seeing the results you expected (the number on the scale is not going down), you need to evaluate what isn't working and make the necessary course correction and try a different approach.

If you are not seeing the results you expected, perhaps look at the type of measurement you are using for the goal you have set. Are you tracking leading indicators and lagging indicators?

Leading indicators are inputs – they are things you can measure as you work towards your goal. Lagging indicators are the outcome of all your inputs. For example if your goal is to lose weight, then your leading indicators would be the number of times you went to the gym for a workout this week, how many sets and reps you did on the weights, the distance you ran on the treadmill. It could also be the type and quantity of food that you consume. The lagging indicator is the outcome of all your inputs – your weight on the scale, your measurements, how you feel – your level of energy.

Another example is if you are in sales, leading indicators would be the number of cold calls you make, the number of face-to-face client meetings you have, or the number of sales presentations you do. The lagging indicator is the result of these activities – More sales!

So as you reflect on the progress of your goals, think about rewording your goals so that you focus more on inputs (leading indicators). By focusing on tracking inputs at the end of the day they should help drive a positive impact on your overall results you are looking to achieve.

What is the best way to track your progress? Write it down in a log or journal.

Robert Craig

Journal – Capture your Brilliance

One of the best ways I have learned to reflect is to capture your activities, progress, thoughts, ideas, problems, solutions into the pages of a journal. I have been journaling for a couple of years now and have developed the positive habit of putting entries into a journal daily.

I start a new journal book at the beginning of the year and in the first few pages define my mission, my vision and goals I would like to achieve for the year. Then, I frequently update my journal and reflect on my progress. I record each day – what were the key activities I completed? What went well during the day – what didn't go well? What are my next steps?

By developing the brilliant habit of recording your life in a journal, you bring more awareness to how you are spending your time. It makes you think and focus on activities that will bring you more value.

In Chapter 3 we talked about energy sources for your light bulb – one of which was gratitude. Writing in your journal and noting daily, 2-3 things that you are thankful for is a great way to add to your happiness and abundance mindset.

A Place to Think about your Brilliance

Taking time to think is critical. Finding a place to think is equally important. I have many places where I take time to think. I think in bed, in the shower, in my den at home, in my living room, in my car, in a quiet office or meeting room.

I look forward to having my quiet time – in an oasis where I can get inside my head and think. This quiet time is where I can think and work on feelings, problems, solutions and ideas. It's during this time that often the proverbial light bulb comes on and provides me with a path forward.

LIGHT Streams of Brilliance

On "The Light Bulb Strategy Blueprint", I have shown various light streams of brilliance that you can reflect on.

One of the light streams of brilliance comes from adding value. What have you done that has added value to another person, a cause, to the world? As Steve Jobs once said, "We're here to put a dent in the universe. Otherwise why else even be here?"

Is the value you have added significant? We all want to feel that the value we add is important. Beyond significance is iconic. To be recognized and remembered for the important value that you have added. To be iconic doesn't necessarily mean that everyone in the world knows your name. It could be that you are iconic in the eyes of another person you have helped, impacted, changed like a child you have raised with lots of love and devotion.

Let me give you a personal experience that happened to me that showed me I was on the right track and making a difference. I came into my home office and found on my desk a hand written letter from my 12 year old son, along with a gift card (to our local coffee place).

Here is what it said:

Dear Father,

I am giving this $15 gift card to you as a token of my gratitude for inspiring me to do great things when it comes to reading, business and strategy and not giving up. I hope that one day I will inspire you and my children as much as you inspired me. Thank you for all you have given me.

Love Nicholas

How did this make me feel? Significant, Important - Brilliant!

Another light stream is the brilliance that comes from your area of expertise. What is it that you determined you would become an expert at? To spend time focused on developing your craft, your talent, your passion. As you devote more time practicing, course correcting, improving your brilliance you move from Expert to Genius and then to Master. Your knowledge is a huge asset to you and all that you connect with. You could lose material things in your life, but you will never lose your brilliance as you become a Master.

A key light stream to reflect on is how you are doing at achieving your goals. Achieving your goals means you are getting done what needs to be done in order that you can realize your vision. Your vision supports your path towards achieving your overall mission in life. Make sure your goals are measurable so you know – yes or no whether you have achieved what you want.

Another light stream reflects on your feelings and overall wellbeing. At the first level we feel pleasure, say from having a great meal, a great conversation, a romantic night out or in. Beyond immediate gratification or pleasure how would you rate your level of happiness? How about your level of overall fulfillment? You need to reflect on this to see if your current course of action is making you feel happy and fulfilled. Is it sustainable?

The Light Bulb Strategy

Of course there are other streams of brilliance that may be very important to you. For example you may have levels of brilliance as it relates to your spirituality and religion. You may define brilliance by the level of income and wealth you have accumulated over time.

LIGHT-Heartedness

As we get close to the end of the book I want to ensure that when you reflect on your progress you aren't too hard on yourself. Having a brilliant life means having fun along the way. You can't take everything so seriously. Know that you will need to make some course corrections along the way – that's just part of the journey to brilliance. Enjoy the process!

Celebration of Light

The other thing to remember is to celebrate your victories as you go through the journey of life.

Celebrate the accomplishment of your goals, even the small ones. You deserve to stop and recognize your accomplishments along the way. By doing so it helps to keep you motivated and keep your momentum going.

Participate and celebrate in the successes that others have achieved. Reflect on their brilliance. Thank them for their contributions.

Be Brilliant, Repeat

The Light Bulb Strategy is a process that repeats. The experience and knowledge you gain along the journey of life helps you grow and develop – it builds your base - your core. It all contributes to further defining WHO you are. As you continue to gain more and more awareness of yourself, you justify that WHAT you are doing is truly WHAT you want to be doing. How do you feel it is going? WHAT you are doing is then supported by your WHY power and your Power Drivers of great health, positive relationships, good fortune and gratitude.

You will be constantly reviewing and course correcting your plan - your plan on HOW you will continue to work towards achieving WHAT you want.

You will protect your time, environment and your mind in order that you can execute your plan and illuminate brilliantly. And execute you must – remember a plan without execution is useless.

The Light Bulb Strategy

Lastly, you will reflect on your experiences, your progress, your brilliance. This is where you decide if things are going well or if course corrections are required.

This brings you back to the beginning of *The Light Bulb Strategy* process again – to build your base. What changes will you make to your light bulb as you continue on your journey to brilliance?

"Think Brilliance. Become Brilliant."

Connect with Me

I hope *The Light Bulb Strategy* has added value to your life. If so, it would be great to hear from you and get your feedback.

If you would like to reach out to me you can connect with me at robert@thelightbulbstrategy.com

- Visit my website:
  www.TheLightBulbStrategy.com

- Attend one of my Light Bulb Strategy courses brought to you through Light Bulb University.

- Invite me for a speaking engagement.

The Light Bulb Strategy™